All You Want
to *Know* But
Didn't Think
You Could *Ask*

All You Want
to *Know* But
Didn't Think
You Could *Ask*

RELIGIONS, CULTS, AND POPULAR BELIEFS

JESSICA L. T. DEVEGA *&* CHRISTINE ORTEGA GAURKEE

THOMAS NELSON
Since 1798

NASHVILLE   DALLAS   MEXICO CITY   RIO DE JANEIRO

Published in Nashville, Tennessee, by Thomas Nelson. Thomas Nelson is a registered trademark of Thomas Nelson, Inc.

Book design and composition by Robin Crosslin

Thomas Nelson, Inc., titles may be purchased in bulk for educational, business, fund-raising, or sales promotional use. For information, please e-mail SpecialMarkets@ThomasNelson.com.

Unless otherwise noted, Scripture quotations are taken from NEW REVISED STANDARD VERSION of the Bible. © 1989 by the Division of Christian Education of the National Council of the Churches of Christ in the U.S.A. All rights reserved.

ISBN: 978-1-4185-4917-6

Printed in the United States of America

15 14 13 12 QG 1 2 3 4 5 6

Contents

Introduction 7

WORLD TRADITIONS 15

Judaism. 17
Christianity. 49
Islam 85
Hinduism. 105
Buddhism. 117
Sikhism. 129
Baha'i. 135
World Traditions Compared 139

RELIGIONS OF PLACE 143

Taoism 145
Shinto 149
Shamanism 153
Confucianism. 157
Zoroastrianism 161
Rastafarianism 167
The Orisha Traditions 171
Nepoaganism, Wicca, and Druidism 177
Native American Religion 181
Religions of Place Compared to Christianity 184

UNIQUELY AMERICAN RELIGIONS 189

Mormonism 191
Unitarian Universalisam 199
Scientology 203
Anabaptist Traditions. 209

Nation of Islam 215
Jehovah's Witness 221
Hare Krishna 225
Uniquely American Traditions Compared
    to Christianity 228

POP CULTURE-BASED RELIGIONS AND BELIEFS . . . 233

Vampirism 235
Jediism 239
Divining, Astrology, Tarot Cards and New Age 243
Belief in the Paranormal and Spirits 247
Demonology and Angelology 251
Fandom 259
Pop Culture-Based Religions Compared
    to Christianity 262

NONRELIGIOUS BELIEFS 265

Atheism 267
Agnosticism 271
Postmodernism 275
Secular Humanism 279
Nonreligious Beliefs Compared to Christianity 282

EXTREMISM 283

Fundamentalism 285
Religious Violence 291
Apocalypticism 303
Charismatic Leadership 311

Conclusion 315

INTRODUCTION

"Someone told me Muslims believe they will be rewarded with seventy-two virgins if they are suicide bombers."

"I heard that Hindus worship cows."

"Did the Jews kill Jesus?"

As teachers of religion for the past decade, we have encountered students with all these comments and many other questions. As with many adults, the teens and young adults we teach have heard at least one common misconception about a religion different from their own. However, when pressed, most people are often unable to identify the exact source of their information. The statements our students make, and the questions they ask about other belief systems, are generally innocent, inquisitive, and almost always based on second or third-hand information.

If you have picked up this book, you probably have questions. You might have heard one of the above statements about other religions and wondered if it was true, or you might have encountered a more insidious or hateful rumor about a tradition other than your own. You may be concerned because you heard someone say that another religion was "violent," "demonic," or "crazy." Perhaps you simply encountered a member of another religion for the very first time and have been wondering what that person believes, how she thinks, how she understands the world, or how to speak to her respectfully while holding true to your own faith.

This book is an attempt to address the sort of questions that people have when learning about another religion for the first time. We don't assume you have any previous knowledge of the religions, cults, and popular beliefs we address in this short book. Instead, we want to give you a concise, general, introductory overview of a wide range of belief systems. It is our hope that by addressing many of the most common stereotypes, misconceptions, and perceptions of religious beliefs around the world that you will come to understand the actual teachings and beliefs of other religious groups and come to a better understanding of your own beliefs and faith and why you hold them.

In this book, we took a closer look at several different types of religious and nonreligious beliefs. It was important to each of us to be as straightforward as possible when writing about each tradition. In that process, we placed objectivity at the center of our writings and approached each belief system, above all, with respect. However, there are some chapters where objectivity is simply difficult. For example, the chapter about religious violence has been written in the style of an academic reporter to present the facts with the hope that we can better understand one another. It goes without saying that we do not encourage or condone any violence, religious or otherwise.

In this book, we strove to gather information that explained the general concepts of each tradition. For us, that included some historical context and information about the origins, founders, people, and important places. Sacred texts often contain the basic beliefs of a tradition and can shed light upon some of the rites, rituals, holidays, and festivals that a religious community holds dear. Therefore, we have included those, when applicable. Furthermore, though historical information and sacred texts may provide a basic structure for understanding a particular tradition, the actual practices of a group are what provide a deeper knowledge about how people behave and interact with the world around them. For this reason, we have noted key practices and important rituals. Our overall hope was that in this book we would be able to provide a concise but rich overview for each tradition.

As teachers, we have met students of many diverse backgrounds and faith traditions, but we are certainly not insiders to most of these belief systems. We have taken the approach of observers, recognizing that we are outsiders. But we hope that our diligent observations may provide insight into people who believe differently than we do, so that we can speak with each other from a position of knowledgeable respect.

The subtitle of this book, "Religions, Cults, and Popular Beliefs," might be confusing. You may wonder what makes a religion different from a cult or popular beliefs. Here are a few general definitions.

By *religion*, we are most often referring to world belief systems such as Judaism, Christianity, Islam, Buddhism, and Hinduism. These systems tend to have well-established worldviews developed over a long period of time. These religions have been historically and geographically influential, often on multiple continents. Religions emphasize tradition, ritual, sacred scripture, structure of belief, and often have centralized authority.

But you will see that some of these characteristics also apply to the newer groups discussed in this book. However, in general the designation *religion* indicates an established tradition with longstanding beliefs and patterns of behavior among followers.

Most people associate the term *cult* with groups that are dangerous or fanatical. Usually, people think of the term *cult* as an insult. However, some scholars in the social sciences—sociology and psychology, for example—use this term in a different way as a very specific designation for a small religious group that often has a less well-established belief systems. These groups tend to be separatist and form around a charismatic leader with unique ideals. Cult leaders often demand high levels of commitment from followers. Some cults are also sects, or splinter groups from a more established religion. Cults need not be inherently abusive or scary, but their isolationism can lead to rumors by outsiders, and can sometimes result in violence from within the group as well as outside the group. In this book, we use the term *cult* in this way. The term is often interchangeable with "new religious movement" or "alternative religion." Some scholars began using these terms in place of *cult* in order to avoid implying that all those groups are dangerous and fanatical.

"Popular beliefs," the third element of the subtitle, is a sort of catch-all category for the purposes of this book. Some popular beliefs, such as atheism or postmodernism, have long histories and established systems of thought. Others, such as vampirism, are more recent and even contradictory in their beliefs and practices.

What unites the diverse groups in this third category is popularity. By this we do not mean that they are the most widely believed or practiced traditions in the world. We simply mean that these groups are common enough that many people might have heard about them or met someone that is a part of one of these groups.

The book is divided into several sections. First, "World Traditions" addresses some of the most influential religions in the world. This includes the Abrahamic traditions: Judaism, Christianity, and Islam. Additionally, "World Traditions" includes Hinduism, which is considered the parent religion of Buddhism, Jainism, and Sikhism. The Baha'i faith is also included in this section. These religions are generally labeled world religions because of the sizes of their populations or their impact on the global community. For example, Judaism has a small world-wide population primarily due to the Holocaust; despite the relatively small size of Judaism it has had a tremendous impact on the world through its influence on and connections to both Christianity and Islam.

The following section, "Religions of Place," considers traditions that are either nature-based or indigenous, meaning that in general these religions are tied to specific geographical regions. For example, Shinto's creation myth includes the story of how the gods created the world, and that Japan came out of that creation. Religious traditions like Santeria, Vodou, and the Rastafari movement are primarily found in the Caribbean islands, where they developed out of oppressive situations related to a history of slavery. Native American and African tribal religions (for example, Yoruba or shamanism) are connected to the land and to a specific community-based understanding of being. However, in the present day, not all so-called indigenous religions are bound to place, as many members of these communities have left their places of origin and have relocated around the world. These include not only traditions like Vodou, Santeria, and Yoruba, but also Taoism, Confucianism, and Zoroastrianism. However, in spite of the fact that these traditions now have global communities in diaspora, the origins, details, and practices still remain connected to the geographical location in which the traditions originated.

Section three is entitled "Uniquely American Traditions." The United States has been called a melting pot, and the analogy of a salad has also been used to express the idea of distinct individuals from various backgrounds all living together on the same land. The freedom of religion guaranteed by the Constitution has fostered the opportunity for many unique religious movements to arise, develop, and flourish in our American "salad." Jehovah's Witnesses, The Church of Jesus Christ of Latter-day Saints, Unitarians, and the Anabaptist traditions all grew out of Christianity, and some still identify themselves as Christians. The Nation of Islam is an offshoot of orthodox Islam; Hare Krishnas come from Hinduism. However, not all the uniquely American traditions are a direct offshoot of a larger tradition. Scientology originated in the United States with help from science fiction author and founder L. Ron Hubbard. All these traditions add to the religious landscape of this pluralistic society.

In recent years, there have been fictional cultural phenomena that have actually influenced the beliefs and identity of real people, whether that is the wizard Harry Potter driving thousands of people to dress in their robes or the Twilight characters motivating girls to save themselves for marriage. The next section of this book, "Pop Culture-Based Religions," addresses various aspects of popular culture that have become religious in either observance or practice. From television fanatics to people seeking to communicate with the paranormal, this portion of the book will cover these wildly popular ideas.

In "Nonreligious Beliefs," we challenge the assumption that all belief is religious. There are some people who hold beliefs that by nature are not religious but that do operate as a system for understanding the world and how humans should interact with it. Whether atheist, agnostic, or postmodern, nonreligious ideologies are on the rise post-September 11.

Since we recognize that religion is observed, practiced, and believed by humans, and that humans are fallible, the final section of the book, "Extremism," discusses some of the worst acts of human behavior prompted by people's religious understandings. Over the course of history, atrocities have been committed in the name of religion; charismatic leaders have encouraged suicide, and apocalyptic traditions have encouraged violence to bring about the end of the world. It is important to address the dangers of what happens when a person's religious understanding causes him or her to do harm to others.

A WORD ABOUT BC AND AD

The traditional way of dividing years is based on the
date of the birth of Jesus. The abbreviation BC stands for
Before Christ, and AD stands for Anno Domini (Latin
for the Year of our Lord). Years before the birth of Jesus
count down to 1 BC; years since count up from 1 AD.
This causes some problems. There is no year 0 in this
calendar system. Second, the BC/AD system was created
by a monk named Dionysius Exiguus, in the sixth century
long before people were able to estimate the year of Jesus'
birth. Historical evidence indicates that Jesus could not
have been born later than 4 BC when Matthew and
Luke's accounts of Jesus' birth are considered together
with other Greek and Latin sources. Matthew 2 mentions
Herod the Great. Luke 2 says that Jesus was born in the
reign of Augustus while Quirinius was governor of Syria.
Obviously, stating that Jesus was born four years "Before
Christ" is linguistically problematic! For this reason,
among others, scholars have taken to using the terms BCE
(Before the Common Era) and CE (Common Era) to refer
to these same time periods. We have chosen to use BCE
and CE in this book to help you become more familiar
with the terminology you will encounter in many history
textbooks.

WORLD
TRADITIONS

Hebrew Bible and tallis, Jewish prayer shawl

JUDAISM

INTRODUCTION

The Jewish faith places a great deal of emphasis on human history as a single, unbroken timeline; that is, Jews believe the world began at one point in the past, it exists now, and one day it will end. While this view might seem familiar, especially to Christians or Muslims who share this view of time, it is quite different from Hindu or Buddhist beliefs in which time is an endless cycle of creation and destruction. Such a worldview means all human beings can draw inspiration and direction from past events. In fact, a central feature of the Jewish faith is a profound connection between present-day practices and ancient stories and promises. To really understand the Jewish faith, then, we must begin with its past.

HISTORY

Origins and Early History

The first place to turn for understanding the origins and early history of Judaism is the Hebrew Bible, or Tanakh (see "Texts").

Hebrew Bible

The Hebrew Bible presents Judaism as always existing, beginning with the creation of the world (Gen. 1–3), and developing over time to include all the elements associated with modern Jewish practice.

In particular, the Torah, or first five books of the Hebrew Bible, provides the most extensive and detailed portrait of the ancient Israelite religion that grew to become Judaism. In many ways, scholars who study Judaism are dependent on the Torah for the history and development of the religion. However, the biblical picture is incomplete; it gives us an idea of the people and concepts which became significant to later Judaism, but the Torah was most likely developed from oral traditions over a long period of time. Most scholars believe that these traditions were not pulled together in written form until between the seventh and fifth centuries BCE. More significantly, the Hebrew Bible is most concerned with the events tied to God's relationship to the chosen people of Israel, so it is often unclear or entirely silent about places, dates, and events connected to the history of Israel's neighbors.

To understand Judaism, one must first understand the history of Israel in the Bible. The Torah begins with Genesis, which traces history beginning with the creation of the world and early human failings (e.g., the first murder [Gen. 4], the Tower of Babel [Gen. 11], and intermarriage with angels [Gen. 6]), and then following the growth and movement of the family of the patriarchs Abraham, Isaac, and Jacob.

God calls Abraham from his homeland to the land of Canaan, which God promises to all of Abraham's male descendants who are circumcised (Gen. 12). Abraham eventually becomes the father of two sons: Ishmael, by Hagar, and Isaac, by Sarah. The Abrahamic religions (Judaism, Christianity, and Islam) trace their spiritual heritage to these patriarchs and matriarchs. God's promise passes to Isaac's son Jacob (later renamed Israel). Jacob/Israel's children (twelve sons and one daughter) settle in the land of Canaan, but they must move to Egypt because of a famine (see Gen. 47).

Israel's history continues in the book of Exodus. Exodus recounts the story of how Jacob's descendants briefly flourished in Egypt before Pharaoh enslaved them. God uses a descendant of Jacob named Moses to bring the Israelites (here called "Hebrews") out of slavery and back to the land promised to their ancestors. As they travel, the people receive a new set of covenant commands, including

The Exodus from Egypt

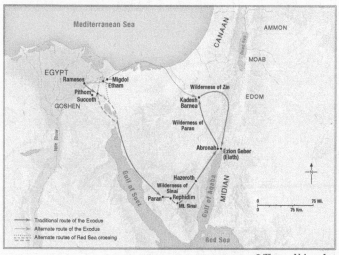

© Thomas Nelson, Inc.

the Ten Commandments (Ex. 20). However, the people are unfaithful to Yahweh (YHWH, the personal name of God given to Moses in Exodus 3:14) and wander for a generation in the wilderness between Egypt and Canaan. The stories of their wanderings make up the remainder of the Torah.

After the death of Moses, God allows the Hebrews to re-enter the land under the leadership of Joshua, who is Moses's second-in-command. A loose confederation of twelve tribes is established in Canaan, led and protected by charismatic male and female warriors called judges. When this system of leadership breaks down, the people demand a king (see 1 Sam. 8). First, Saul is appointed

Settlement of the Tribes

© GeoNova

The Divided Kingdom

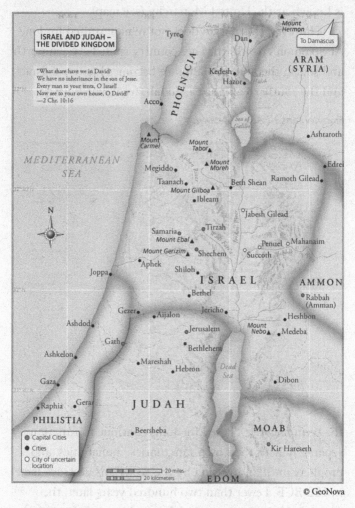

**ISRAEL AND JUDAH –
THE DIVIDED KINGDOM**

"What share have we in David?
We have no inheritance in the son of Jesse.
Every man to your tents, O Israel!
Now see to your own house, O David!"
—2 Chr. 10:16

To Damascus

ARAM (SYRIA)

AMMON

ISRAEL

JUDAH

MOAB

EDOM

PHILISTIA

PHOENICIA

MEDITERRANEAN SEA

Dead Sea

Sea of Galilee

- ● Capital Cities
- ● Cities
- ○ City of uncertain location

20 miles
20 kilometers

© GeoNova

as king, then David, who adopts the Jebusite city of Jerusalem as his capital. David's son Solomon succeeds his father, and during his rule, the first temple is built in Jerusalem. For more information on the religious significance of the temple, see "Major Beliefs." This period is known as the United Monarchy (see map).

However, this nation does not remain united for long. At Solomon's death, the tiny country splits between north and south; the northern alliance becomes known as Israel, and the southern alliance as Judah, from which we get

Babylonians Invade Palestine

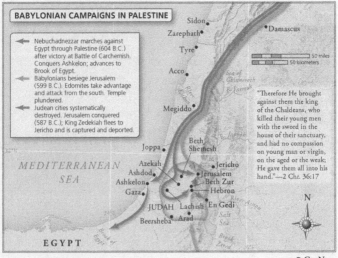

© GeoNova

the term *Judaism*. These kingdoms continue to function separately with their own sanctuaries, monarchies, and prophets until an invasion by the Assyrians destroys Israel in 722 BCE. Fewer than two hundred years later, the neo-Babylonians capture Judah and destroy Solomon's Temple in Jerusalem, ending the monarchic period in the south and sending the Judahites into exile in Babylon. The people live in exile for nearly fifty years before the Persian king Cyrus allows them to return to Jerusalem.

Upon their return, the Judahites rebuild a second temple in Jerusalem, and here the history of the Jewish people as told in the Bible draws to a close.

Archaeology

It is interesting to note that, in contrast to this lengthy biblical history, the archaeological evidence of the origins and development of Judaism is rather sparse. The earliest attested use of the name Israel outside the Bible appears in the thirteenth century BCE, when an Egyptian pharaoh named Merneptah recorded his conquest of a people called Israel. The date upon Merneptah's victory stela (an upright column of stone with markings or writing) might correspond with the time of the settlement under Joshua mentioned in the Bible. However, the stela itself provides no useful details about who the conquered people were, nor where they originated. Similarly, the establishment and extent of Jerusalem as the City of David is difficult to verify from archaeology, and no evidence of the Solomonic Temple remains, even though modern forgeries pop up for sale occasionally.

However, even with limited physical evidence, it is apparent that the Jewish people have a lengthy past in and around the land of Israel. Additionally, when these archaeological clues are taken together with the biblical text, we get a clearer picture of the beliefs which became central to Judaism.

BELIEFS

One God

Judaism is a monotheistic religion. The Jewish belief in one personal God who makes covenants with humankind appears throughout the Hebrew Bible. In Deuteronomy 6:4, for example, the Jewish people find an affirmation of this monotheistic faith: "Hear [Shema] O Israel, the Lord is your God, the Lord is One."

The Shema is more than just an affirmation of the singleness of God. It discloses the personal name of God as well. The Tetragrammaton (four letters) YHWH, which in English is translated as "Lord" and scholars pronounce "Yahweh," is the proper name of God, revealed to Moses at the burning bush (see "Origins and Early History"). Many Jews believe that YHWH is too holy to speak. Instead they will substitute the title Adonai ("Lord") when YHWH appears in the Hebrew text. Some Jews will not write out the word *God* and instead choose to write *G–d* as a sign of reverence.

Covenant

The Shema conveys belief in the covenant, which is a unique arrangement between God and humanity, and which is a foundational belief in Judaism. Covenants in the Bible include the Abrahamic covenant (Gen. 11) and the Mosaic covenant (Ex. 20), among others. These two covenants provide a significant basis for Jewish ritual practices and beliefs about sacred space. Both covenants are conditional; that is, they are "if–then" covenants in which both sides are expected to do something in order to receive something else. The Abrahamic covenant, for example, promises the patriarch a land (Canaan) and numerous descendants if all male members of the community are circumcised. Likewise, the Mosaic covenant is an extensive collection of interpersonal, sacrificial, and communal commands which allow the Jewish people to live in a unique relationship with God.

Obedience to God's Torah

Adherence to the Mosaic commandments revealed in the Torah is another distinctive feature of Jewish belief. The word *Torah* refers to the commandments themselves, the first five books of the Hebrew Bible collectively (see "Texts"), and the interpretation of these commandments in later Judaism (often called Oral Torah). The Torah commandments are a series of rules concerning diet and propriety known as kosher law, or kashrut. For example, Levitical law commands believers to abstain from eating pork, shellfish, and other "unclean" foods (Lev. 11). The law also forbids mixing fibers (Lev. 19), having contact with dead bodies (Lev. 15), or touching items that have been in contact with a menstruating woman (Lev. 21).

To outsiders, these may seem like arbitrary rules, but in the context of Judaism, they provide structure, stability, and a sense of purpose to even the most mundane daily tasks. Additionally, much like circumcision, the kosher laws are a visible reminder of the distinction between those within God's covenant community and those who are outside of it (called Gentiles). The covenant commandments related to kosher law remain significant for many Jewish people today, especially Orthodox,

The Assyrian Empire (650 b.c.)

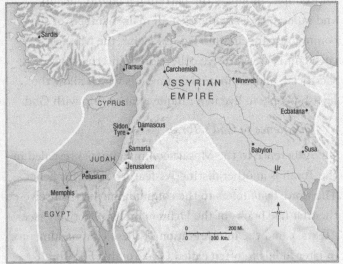

© Thomas Nelson, Inc.

Ultra-Orthodox, Hasidic, and some Conservative groups (see "Groups").

The Land

Though not necessarily a belief, a deep reverence for the land promised to Abraham and his descendants is a respect which many Jewish people share. This land, known as Canaan, and subsequently called Israel or Palestine, changed hands many times over the millennia because of its strategic geographical position amidst major world powers who wished to control access to Asia, Europe, and Africa. For the Jewish people, however, the land was theologically significant; not only did the land have connections to the covenant with Abraham, but Israel also contained Jerusalem, the city of David.

Jerusalem has religious significance to Christians and Muslims as well, but for Jewish people the city is most notable as the site of the first and second temples.

The Temple

Solomon's Temple

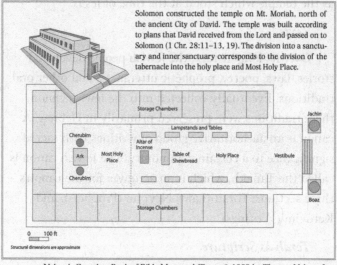

Solomon constructed the temple on Mt. Moriah, north of the ancient City of David. The temple was built according to plans that David received from the Lord and passed on to Solomon (1 Chr. 28:11–13, 19). The division into a sanctuary and inner sanctuary corresponds to the division of the tabernacle into the holy place and Most Holy Place.

Storage Chambers

Jachin

Lampstands and Tables

Cherubim

Altar of Incense

Ark

Most Holy Place

Table of Shewbread

Holy Place

Vestibule

Cherubim

Boaz

Storage Chambers

0   100 ft

Structural dimensions are approximate

Nelson's Complete Book of Bible Maps and Charts © 1993 by Thomas Nelson, Inc.

The first temple, built by King Solomon, stood for over four hundred years (see "History"). This first temple was a symbol of Zion, the covenantal belief that YHWH dwelled uniquely in the temple and protected the land ruled by an everlasting Davidic monarchy. The belief in Zion persisted even after the first temple was destroyed and the Jewish people were exiled by the Neo-Babylonians. However, the meaning of Zion shifted to refer to a future reality in which the people would celebrate the restoration of the Davidic monarchy. The second temple, begun under the rule of Persian king Cyrus in approximately 536 BCE and expanded during the Greek and Roman occupations, was eventually destroyed by the Roman army in 70 CE. The remaining western wall of this second temple is a pilgrimage site for Jewish people, as well as for Christians who remember it as the temple which stood at the time of Jesus.

Texts

Over its long history, the Jewish people developed stories, laws, poetry, prophetic utterances, and other oral traditions. Eventually collected into the Jewish canon, these traditions were preserved primarily in Hebrew. A canon is an authoritative group of writings with sacred significance to a certain community. The Jewish canon is called the Tanakh, which is an acronym for the canon's three sections: Torah (Law), Nevi'im (Prophets), and Ketuvim (Writings).

Torah as Scripture

The Torah is the first section of the Hebrew Bible, and it contains the books of Genesis, Exodus, Leviticus, and Deuteronomy. While "Torah" usually translates as "law," and while the last three books in the Torah contain large sections of covenantal law given to Moses, not everything in the Torah is legal code. This section of the Hebrew Bible also contains stories of human origins, patriarchs and matriarchs, the liberation of the Hebrew slaves from Egypt, and much more. For Jews, the Torah is central to their faith; it is so important to Jewish identity that over the course of a given year, the entire text of the Torah will be read in the synagogue.

The second section of the Hebrew Bible, called Nevi'im, contains books that Christians categorize as historical narratives (Joshua, Judges, Samuel, and Kings) and prophetic books (Isaiah, Jeremiah, Micah, etc.). The events in the Nevi'im roughly correspond with the period during which the Jewish people were "in the land" of Canaan, first as a confederation of twelve tribes, then as a united kingdom, and finally as a divided kingdom besieged by foreign powers. However, scholars think that the prophetic books were collected and preserved in written form well after the events described, probably around the time of the Babylonian Exile (see "Origins and Early History").

The Ketuvim, the final collection of the Tanakh, is also the most literarily diverse. The books of the Ketuvim include poetry (Psalms, Song of Songs), wisdom literature (Proverbs, Ecclesiastes), and short stories (Esther, Ruth), among others. This third category also includes works which were reclassified in the Christian canon as historical or prophetic works, such as the Chronicles and Daniel. Taken with the Torah and Nevi'im, the Ketuvim completes the collection of the twenty-four books which comprise Jewish sacred Scripture.

Rituals

As with so many aspects of Judaism, central rituals and rites of passage are related to significant events in biblical history. Some rituals are sacred events that are repeated daily, weekly, monthly, or yearly. Other important **rites** are events which occur only once in a person's lifetime.

Practices

Daily ritual emphasizes the covenantal relationship with God that is so important to Judaism. Keeping kosher, or distinguishing between clean and unclean foods and behaviors, is based on the Mosaic Law. Daily prayer rituals include recitation of the Shema from the book of Deuteronomy and wearing yarmulkes (head coverings), tefillin (leather pouches containing the Torah), and tallit (square shawls) which are fringed at the corners with tzitzit (see picture). The wearing of these items is based on Torah commandments in Numbers 15:38–40 and Deuteronomy 6:8. While daily prayers can be performed individually, groups will often gather at the synagogue for collective daily prayer. A minyan, or minimum of ten adults (men only in Orthodox synagogues), is necessary for this type of prayer.

Holy Days

The most important weekly ritual in Judaism is the celebration of the Sabbath, or day of rest. The Sabbath recalls the first Genesis creation story, in which God rested after six days of creating the universe (Gen. 2:3–4). Since that story describes the days of creation as beginning in the evening, the Sabbath begins at nightfall on Friday and lasts until dusk Saturday.

After welcoming the Sabbath Friday evening with a family meal, a blessing, and the lighting of candles, observant Jews devote themselves to prayer and worship, and refrain from work, in accordance with another Torah commandment (Ex. 20:8–10). The definition of what constitutes "work" varies, however. For some people, refraining from work means spending time with family and engaging in Torah study while still enjoying modern conveniences; others define work strictly, and they abstain from using appliances, driving, cooking, and even pushing elevator buttons. One's understanding of what constitutes work, as well as when Sabbath worship is held, is most often related to the group within Judaism to which one belongs (see "Groups").

Most yearly rituals are related to biblical mandates as well. The Jewish religious year begins in the fall, with the celebration of Rosh Hashanah (meaning "Head of the Year"). In the Bible, Rosh Hashanah is called the Day of Blowing Horns (Lev. 23:24; Num. 29:1). In a modern-day synagogue service, the shofar (ram's horn) is still blown to call the people to a time of reflection upon the misdeeds of the previous year. Ten days of contemplation, reflection, and repentance follow Rosh Hashanah, leading to Yom Kippur (the Day of Atonement). Yom Kippur is also described in the Torah as a day to "afflict your souls" (Lev. 16:29). Yom Kippur services last throughout the day, and activities include reading the book of Jonah and praying for forgiveness and reconciliation with God. People often fast for the entire day, from sunset to sunset, even refraining from drinking water, as a sign of their repentance. Together, these two days constitute the Days of Awe, the most important holy days of the religious year.

Passover, another yearly ritual, is celebrated in the spring. This day remembers the exodus from Egypt (see

"History"). While the Days of Awe emphasize synagogue worship, Passover is more family-oriented and focuses on a seder meal at the home. Over the course of the meal, the events of Exodus are recounted both verbally and through the food. The seder plate (see picture), a central feature at the dinner, traditionally includes a lamb shank, representing the lamb's blood painted on the doorframes of Hebrew houses on the night of the first Passover; an egg, symbolizing new life; bitter herbs, commemorating the bitterness of Egyptian slavery; charoset, an apple, and cinnamon chutney, representing the mortar used for building while the Hebrews were enslaved; and a green vegetable like parsley dipped in salt water, remembering the tears of the enslaved. Along with these traditional foods, the story of the liberation is retold in the form of questions and answers, with a young child inquiring of the adults what makes the Passover night "different from all other nights."

While these three holy days constitute the major celebrations of the Jewish year, non-Jews (especially in the United States) are probably most familiar with Hanukah, the winter festival of lights. It is important for non-Jews to recognize that Hanukah is not a Jewish version of Christmas, although the two holidays often occur at the same time of year. Instead, Hanukah is a holiday of political and religious liberation, recalling a story in the books of the Maccabees about a rebellion under Greek rule in 164 BCE (see "Post-Biblical Judaism"). The Maccabees are important Jewish historical writings that are not in the Tanakh, but which do appear in the Christian Apocrypha. When the Greek army desecrated

Expansion of Palestine Under the Maccabees

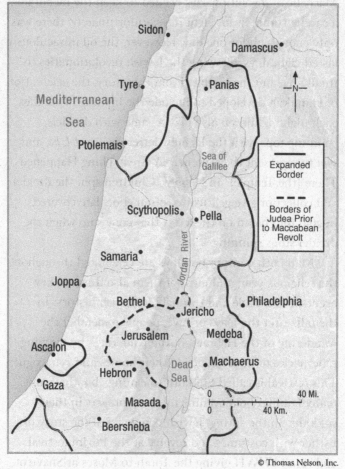

© Thomas Nelson, Inc.

the second temple by making unclean offerings to Zeus, a group of faithful Jews retook the temple and protected it long enough to rededicate it to God. In fact, the word *Hanukah* means "rededication."

To make the temple a sacred place again, the Maccabean revolutionaries needed to keep the menorah, a candle stand, lit for eight days; unfortunately, there was only enough oil for one day. However, the oil miraculously lasted eight days, allowing the Jewish revolutionaries to finally reclaim the temple. From this story, the celebration of Hanukah developed to include the lighting of candles each night. Children also play a game with dreidels, spinning tops with the Hebrew letters *nun*, *gadol*, *he*, and *shin* to represent the sentence "A Great Thing Happened There [the Temple]" in Hebrew. Children spin the dreidel and collect or give gelt (coins, often chocolate covered in gold foil) based on the letter that comes up when the dreidel stops spinning.

Many other minor holidays are celebrated throughout the religious year, and most of them also draw on key events in the Bible and throughout Jewish history. In the fall, after the Days of Awe, people remember the wandering of the Hebrews in the wilderness by pitching tabernacles or booths outside their homes and synagogues. This festival is called Sukkoth (meaning "booths") and many families hold evening meals or prayers in their sukkahs. In the spring, Jewish people retell the story of Esther with costumes and revelry at the Purim festival and recall YHWH giving the Torah to Moses at Shavu'ot.

Rites

Whereas a Jewish person might celebrate holy days many times, other rituals are performed only once to mark transitions from one stage of life to the next. These events are called rites of passage, and they begin for the Jewish person shortly after birth. Eight days after a baby boy is born, Jewish families will hold a bris milah, or covenant of circumcision. A specially trained person called a mohel performs the bris, either in a synagogue or in the family's home. In some Jewish families, a naming ceremony for girls, called Simchat Bat or Brit Bat, is also performed within the first month of the baby's life.

When a child grows to an appropriate age to take on the religious obligations of the Torah for himself or herself, a second rite of passage occurs: the Bar or Bat Mitzvah. The word *mitzvah* means commandment, and in this coming-of-age rite a youth (usually about 13 years old) is declared responsible for the commandments of the Torah. In most bar or bat mitzvot, the youth will read in Hebrew a portion of the Torah which she or he has prepared with the help of the synagogue's rabbi and cantor. The cantor is the person who sings the Scriptures in a synagogue service. Historically, only young men have participated in a bar mitzvah (meaning "son of the covenant"), and this remains true in Orthodox Jewish communities (see "Groups"). However, some Jewish communities have begun to celebrate a similar rite for young women (the bat mitzvah, or "daughter of the covenant").

Marriage is also a rite of passage in Judaism. In the marriage rite, the couple is often married under a chuppah, or canopy, which represents the new home the couple will share and recalls the story of Rebecca and Isaac, in which a couple was married when he took her into his mother's tent (Gen. 24:67). The ceremony includes an exchange of vows and rings, as in many other religious traditions, but also includes signing a ketubah (marriage

Alexander's Greek Empire

(Daniel 2, 7, 8, 11)

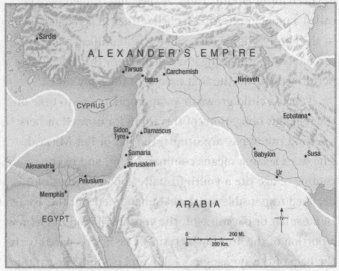

© Thomas Nelson, Inc.

contract) and stomping on a glass at the conclusion of the service. This last tradition is of disputed origin, but some people believe that the shattered glass is to remind the assembly that, even while great joy is celebrated, the temple is still in ruins.

The solemnity of death is also marked by several traditional Jewish practices. When a member of the community dies, family members will sit shiva for seven days, receiving guests and remembering the life of the departed. A family member sitting shiva will cover all mirrors to avoid vanity while focusing on the life of the deceased, wear no shoes, sit on low stools, and tear at the edges or pockets of her or his clothes. This last practice is in keeping with the biblical tradition of tearing, or rending, one's garments when mourning.

Post-Biblical Judaism

Judaism's biblical history ends with the building of the second temple because that is the latest historical event mentioned in the Jewish Scripture. This temple became a central theme in the next five hundred years of post-biblical Judaism, spanning the Persian, Greek, and Roman conquests of Palestine. The refurbished temple became a source of conflict for both Greece and Rome, leading to rebellion and, ultimately, to destruction.

In the middle of the third century BCE, Alexander the Great extended Greek rule over the Judean countryside, which resulted in the spreading of Greek culture and values (called Hellenism) to the lands he conquered, including Judea. Hellenistic values were not well received by many Jews, as they conflicted with monotheism (see "Beliefs"). In the 100s BCE, local Greek leaders in Judea were adamant that the Jewish people must submit to Hellenistic values; this included remaining uncircumcised, eating unclean foods in violation of kosher laws, and worshipping Greek gods. According to the Maccabees, the second century Greek leader Antiochus IV demanded that the Jews call him Epiphanes ("God made manifest") and instructed his army to sacrifice a pig to Zeus in the holiest part of the Jewish Temple. Such a desecration was horrifying to many Jews, who rebelled and took back the temple to try to make it holy again. These events formed the foundation for the miraculous rededication of the temple commemorated during Hanukkah (see "Practices and Holy Days").

The cleansing of the temple marked the beginning of a brief period of independence, called the Hasmonean Period. During this time, the Maccabean family who led the revolt against Hellenism established a priesthood at the temple and became an authority. This period lasted until the Hasmoneans allied themselves with Rome, eventually falling again under foreign occupation by 63 BCE.

Under Roman rule, the official policy toward Judaism was one of tolerance because of Judaism's status as an ancient religion. However, in practice Rome often persecuted the Jewish people for sedition and their failure to worship the emperor. Unsurprisingly, Jewish people began to articulate a belief in a Messiah who would liberate them from Roman oppression. The word *messiah* is from the Hebrew word *mashiakh*, which means "anointed one." This messianic hope reflected a desire to return to the anointed, chosen rule of the Davidic line. Messianism became closely tied to apocalypticism, or the belief that a world controlled by evil would be overcome by good and be made new under the rule of God's chosen Messiah. Some Jewish people saw themselves as living in this apocalyptic time, and sought to overturn Roman rule violently. In response to numerous rebellions between 60 BCE and 60 CE, the Roman army laid siege to Jerusalem and destroyed the second temple in 70 CE.

The temple was not rebuilt, and shortly after its destruction, the Romans dispersed the Jewish people from their homeland. During this period of diaspora,

Jews settled into communities in Europe, Asia, and North Africa. In the places, people reimagined Judaism. Previously, Judaism had emphasized certain beliefs and practices related to the temple, as outlined in the Torah. For example, Jews commonly made pilgrimage to the temple and performed sacrifices with the assistance of temple priests, with reverence for the presence of God within the Holy of Holies inside the temple. However, after 70 CE, Judaism needed to adapt to a world without the Jerusalem temple. Synagogues, or gathering spaces for worship and prayer, became more important. The Torah took on a more central place, and interpreters of the Torah were given greater authority. These teachers, called rabbis, became the key leaders of post-Second Temple Judaism, so the diaspora period is often also called the beginning of rabbinic Judaism.

During this period, rabbis made two key contributions to modern Judaism: the final canonization of the Tanakh (see "Texts"), and the development of Torah interpretations known as Mishnah and Talmud over several subsequent centuries. These interpretations helped Judaism continue to thrive in the diaspora because they made the Scripture relevant to believers, regardless of where or when they might live. The rabbis helped diaspora Jews know how to observe the Sabbath rest. They answered people's questions about why God demanded Abraham's sacrifice of Isaac.

Two other religious traditions developed from Judaism's sacred text and belief in monotheism. Christianity grew from a sect of Judaism that believed Jesus of Nazareth was the Messiah. After the destruction of the temple, these two groups began a process of separating from each other with Christianity emphasizing the inclusion of Gentiles (non-Jewish people) and developing their own Scripture (the Christian New Testament). As Christianity grew in prominence and became the official religion of the Roman Empire, many Christians began to regard the Jewish people as heretics based on a faulty interpretation of the Christian Gospel of Matthew. Christians commonly attacked their Jewish neighbors in pogroms, fueled by a belief in false rumors that Jewish people murdered Christians or caused the Black Plague. Many Jewish people were deported from Christian-controlled lands, or forced to live in small communities called ghettos.

Islam is another religion that recognizes the same God and prophets as Judaism, and Islam draws many of its traditions from Jewish and Christian non-canonical traditions that circulated in Arabia. As Islam spread from the Middle East into Europe and North Africa, it, too, had an impact on diaspora Judaism. In general, the interaction between Judaism and Islam was more peaceful than that of Judaism and Christianity. In Spain, for example, Muslims ruled with toleration over the Jewish population for nearly 700 years beginning in 711 CE. Peaceful coexistence ended with the rise of Christian rule and subsequent expulsion or forced conversion of Muslims.

As Judaism moved into the modern era, Jewish leaders began to question how best to encounter the modern world. Some, like Moses Mendelssohn (1729–86), asked Jews to embrace modernity and become active participants in the philosophy, scholarship, science, and cultural activities of Europeans. In so doing, he believed the Jewish people would avoid being left behind or further segregated from their Christian neighbors. Others disagreed, however, calling Jews to maintain traditional interpretations of biblical commands and to resist integrating into Gentile society. Samson Raphael Hirsch (1808–88) was one such traditionalist. From these two very different views came two different sects: Reform and (neo) Orthodox Judaism (see "Groups").

However they decided to approach modernity, Jewish people still found relationships with their neighbors in Europe difficult and bitter, if not outright hateful. The Holocaust under Hitler's regime during World War II is the best-known example of **anti-Semitism** (anti-Jewish sentiment and actions) during the twentieth century. However, even before the Holocaust, Jews throughout Europe were being herded into ghettos, facing accusations that they carried disease or conspired to destroy Christian communities. Additionally, European Christians continued to brand Jews as heretics and Christ-killers. Jews suffered economically and lacked political redress in most European nations. Thus, the Holocaust might be seen as the culmination of a centuries-long hatred—the worst example among many. Still, the Holocaust, in which millions of Jews were murdered by the Nazi regime, was a wake-up call for Europeans and Americans who failed to act on their behalf. From this horrific event came a collective will on the part of the Western world to protect the Jewish people from future atrocities, and the result was the creation of the modern state of Israel.

As previously noted, the Jewish people had been forcibly removed from Palestine under Roman rule, and had moved into the wider Mediterranean world. However, as persecution in Europe grew, many Jews called for a return to this homeland, and the reestablishment of a Jewish state there. Theodor Herzl (1860–1904) was among the first to publicly promote Zionism, a movement supporting the organization of an independent Jewish homeland centered on Jerusalem. After World War II, and the horrors of the Holocaust, international sentiment was such that the time was right to realize Herzl's dream. In 1948, England turned over its Palestinian protectorate, and the United Nations declared it the modern State of Israel.

Of course, this piece of property was not uninhabited at the time of its new designation by the United Nations. Christians had been living there since the first century CE, and Muslims since the seventh century; both claimed Jerusalem as a holy city, as did the Jews. By turning the lands over to the new Israel, many Christian and Muslim Palestinians were displaced and forced to seek refuge in camps or in adjoining countries. As a result, conflict has continued over the existence of Israel, the control of Jerusalem, and the rights of the Muslim and Christian refugees still living in camps.

DEMOGRAPHICS

Groups

As Judaism developed over many centuries, multiple ways of practicing the religion also developed. We have already seen how the Jewish faith adapted to the destruction of the two temples, the needs of the diaspora, persecution in Europe, immigration, and the development of the state of Israel. These adaptations sometimes also resulted in formal divisions or the creation of separate sects—smaller groups with unique beliefs or practices. While it would be very difficult to describe all the diversity that currently exists in Judaism, below are four of the largest groups, along with brief descriptions of what makes each unique.

Orthodox Judaism claims to have the longest continuous history out of all the Jewish groups, drawing upon the Torah and the rabbinic Judaism that developed after the destruction of the second temple. Orthodox Jews practice strict interpretation of the Torah, keeping its commandments as literally as possible. For example, the directives to keep kosher and to rest on the Sabbath are held reverently. In the synagogue, men and women sit separately to avoid distraction during prayer, and women are not allowed to be rabbis. Sabbath worship is held on Saturday, and the service is entirely in Hebrew.

Smaller groups exist within Orthodox Judaism. Hasidism, a form of Ultra-Orthodox belief, developed in the 1800s in Europe under the guidance of Baal Shem Tov (a title, meaning "master of the good name") who insisted that Judaism look inward. Strict observance of the law, he believed, remained a central feature of Jewish life, but a mystical emphasis—focused on loving God with the whole heart and responding joyfully to that love—was also important. Thus, Hasidic Judaism today is deeply committed to Orthodox practice, while at the same time is devoted to a deep personal communion with God. Many Hasidic Jews have moved to the modern state of Israel as a reflection of their belief that the Messiah will one day arrive to claim the city of Jerusalem and establish a new temple there.

Reform Judaism developed out of the European Enlightenment. Confronted with the challenges of modernity, many Jews came to believe that the claims of the Hebrew Bible and Talmud could no longer be sustained. Moses Mendelssohn most famously articulated these beliefs, calling for reform among the Jews of Europe in order to better integrate with their Christian neighbors. Since that time, Reform Jews have continued this tradition of integration and change, and many of these changes are evident in worship. For example, synagogues in the Reform tradition use almost no Hebrew in worship, choosing instead the vernacular, the common language of the surrounding community. Worship is held Friday evening, and men and women sit together, unlike in Orthodox worship. The Reform tradition in the United States was also the first Jewish community in America to ordain women in 1972. In terms of ritual practice, Reform Jews generally do not keep kosher, do permit certain work on the Sabbath, and do not look for a coming political Messiah or the rebuilding of the temple in Jerusalem. The Reform tradition contains the largest group of Jews in Europe and the United States.

Some Jews in the United States, however, believed Reform Judaism changed too much from Orthodox tradition, while at the same time recognizing that many older beliefs and practices were limiting in the modern world. These Jews, under the leadership of Sabato Morais, developed the Jewish Theological Seminary in New York City, and this seminary has been the center for a third movement, Conservative Judaism. Conservative Jews seek a middle ground between the perceived extremes of both Orthodox and Reform groups, stating that biblical law is both eternal and changeable.

A more recent development is a fourth group called Reconstructionist Judaism, begun in the 1920s in the United States under the leadership of Rabbi Mordecai Kaplan. The Reconstructionist Jewish community seeks to reclaim and emphasize the cultural contributions of Jewish people. Kaplan famously stated that tradition (like Torah or rabbinic interpretation) has "a vote but not a veto." Thus, while recognizing the Torah and its important historical influence on Jewish culture, a Reconstructionist does not feel obligated to keep its commands. Instead, Reconstructionism emphasizes the importance of the community and of sharing in the inherited culture of the Jewish people.

UNDERSTANDING JUDAISM

A profound sense of history, above all, gives Jewish people their identity and belief system. The main text of Judaism, the Tanakh, retells the very oldest histories of the people, and connects to that history current beliefs and practices. Throughout its history, the Jewish faith has encountered many challenges and difficulties, and over time has changed from a temple-focused religion to a rabbinic religion. In the modern era, the experience of persecution and the Holocaust has given rise to a renewed emphasis on the importance of the land of Israel. Certainly, the past has made Judaism what it is today.

FOR FURTHER READING

Finkelstein, Israel and Amihai Mazar. *The Quest for the Historical Israel: Debating Archaeology and the History of Early Israel*. Atlanta: Society of Biblical Literature Press, 2007.

The Jewish Bible: Tanakh: The Holy Scriptures. Philadelphia: Jewish Publication Society, 2003.

Kaplan, Mordecai. *Judaism as a Civilization: Toward a Reconstruction of American-Jewish Life*. Philadelphia: Jewish Publication Society, 2010.

Lundquist, John M. *The Temple of Jerusalem: Past, Present, and Future*. Westport, CT: Greenwood Publishing, 2008.

Neusner, Jacob. *A Short History of Judaism: Three Meals, Three Epochs*. Minneapolis: Augsburg Fortress, 1992.

Shermer, Michael and Alex Gobman. *Denying History: Who Says the Holocaust Never Happened and Why Do They Say It?* Los Angeles: University of California Press, 2000.

Strassfeld, Michael, et al. *The Jewish Holidays: A Guide and Commentary*. New York: Harper and Row, 1985.

*Clergyman
holding Eucharist*

CHRISTIANITY

INTRODUCTION

Christianity developed out of Judaism, and the two traditions continue to share much in common. However, over Christianity's 2,000-year history, Christians have established many new beliefs, practices, scriptures, and traditions. Today, while there are some common ideals which unite the tradition, Christianity is marked much more by diversity than uniformity. This chapter will address the rich diversity of Christian beliefs and practices, where they originated, and what impact this diversity has on believers today.

HISTORY

Judea under Roman Control

The Roman Empire at the time of Jesus's birth was vast and exceedingly powerful. Rome controlled the territories surrounding the Mediterranean, extending into Africa, Europe, and the Middle East. Among the protectorates of the Empire was a small strip of land along the easternmost edge of the sea; this land, which was called Judea, was historically important to the Jewish people as it housed their holy temple in the capital city of Jerusalem. Rome ruled over this protectorate as it did most of the rest of its empire; obedience to the emperor was expected, and acts of rebellion were severely punished.

The Jewish people living in Judea struggled with Roman demands for obedience. In Rome, civic duty was equated with religious reverence toward the emperor. Because Jews were strict monotheists, worshipping the emperor or using coins bearing his picture were forms of idolatry. Furthermore, Roman control over Jerusalem interfered with a scriptural covenant stating that a king from David's line would someday reign there. For this reason, the Jewish people imagined a coming day in which Roman rule would end, and an anointed messiah-king would usher in a new kingdom ordained by God.

The Life of Jesus

Information about the life of Jesus was not written down during his lifetime, in part because of this messianic expectation. Those who believed that Jesus was the Messiah relied on oral rather than written communication to share this conviction, since they thought the end of this world was fast approaching, and the spoken word could reach greater numbers of people. However, when the first generation that knew Jesus began to die, and the expected eschaton (end of the world) did not come, believers began to collect stories of Jesus's life, teachings, and death into gospels. The word "gospel" is related to the Greek world *euangelion*, or "good news." Eventually, Christians canonized only a few of these gospels, giving final authority to four such books out of the many which were produced during the first few centuries of Christianity (see "Sacred Texts").

Only two of the canonical gospels—Luke and Matthew—tell of Jesus's birth. These two accounts differ

The Land of the Gospels

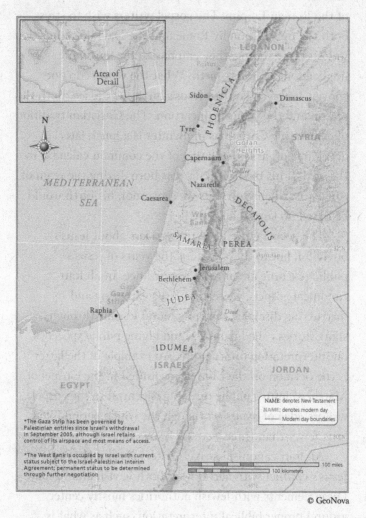

© GeoNova

in many details, but they also share some common themes: Jesus is born in Bethlehem, the city of David; his parents are Mary and Joseph, the latter of whom is of the lineage of David; and his birth coincides with a Roman census, conducted for tax purposes in the outer regions of the Roman Empire. The gospel writers wish to stress both the persecution by Rome and the Davidic connection to Jesus; in so doing, they emphasize the messianic implications of Jesus's birth. What the writers do not convey, however, is when Jesus's birth took place. Both the season and the year are uncertain. The Christian tradition of celebrating Christmas midwinter is a much later development, as is the dating of the common calendar to the year of his birth. If Jesus was born during the reign of Augustus, when Quirinius was governor, his birth would be dated no later than 4 BCE.

The gospel writers tell us even less about Jesus's boyhood, but to these writers, the years of Jesus's public teaching are of great importance. In all four canonical gospels, we read of Jesus gathering and instructing disciples, teaching moral lessons through short stories called parables, and giving public speeches on interpretation of Scripture. An example of the latter is the Sermon on the Mount, recounted in the Gospel of Matthew. Jesus's public teaching is central to the gospel writers' idea of *euangelion* though the whole period likely lasts fewer than three years of Jesus's life.

All four canonical gospel writers also emphasize Jesus's conflict with authorities, both Jewish and Roman. Disagreements with Jewish authorities mostly center around proper biblical interpretation, such as what is lawful to do on the Sabbath (Mark 2:23–28), or what is the nature of resurrection (Matt. 22:23–30). Jesus's conflict with Rome, however, is political. Any messianic claims could result in his death, since it would be akin to Jesus appointing himself king over Judea, therefore being a traitor to Rome. Indeed, at his crucifixion, the sign displaying the charge against him reads, "King of the Jews" (Mark 15:26). Given the method of his execution, Jesus clearly is killed as a traitor; crucifixion was not a punishment for religious offenses in Jesus's time; instead, it was a particularly cruel means of execution the Romans used to both torture the victim and serve as graphic, public warning to any who might follow the traitor's example.

However, the story of Jesus does not end at his crucifixion. All four of the canonical gospel writers include stories of an empty tomb, and most include appearances of Jesus to his disciples three or more days after his execution. These resurrection stories become a central feature of Christian belief. The resurrection of the dead at the time of judgment is already a common Jewish idea at this time, but for the early Christians, Jesus's resurrection has added significance. It becomes a symbol of God's power over death, the coming end of the world, and—for some Christians—the end of the sacrificial system at the temple. Early Christians remember the Resurrection by meeting to worship on the first day of the week, a practice which still continues to this day.

From Judaism to Christianity

Many of Jesus's followers took the message of his life, teaching, and resurrection out into the Roman world. They claimed that Jesus was the Messiah, though a different kind of messiah than Jews expected at this point in history. They further claimed that his death and

The Roman Empire in New Testament Times

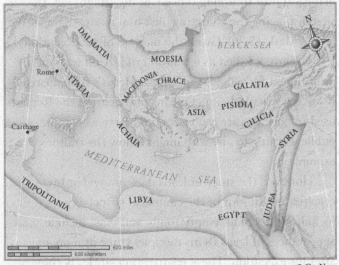

© GeoNova

resurrection marked the beginning of a new age, and that the final judgment of humanity would soon be upon the world. These people were called apostles, or "sent ones." Among them was a man who never knew Jesus during his lifetime, but who claimed to have received a special revelation of the risen Jesus. His name was Saul of Tarsus, otherwise known as Paul.

At first, Paul was an opponent of the new Christians. He writes that he persecuted Christians because he believed them to be heretics for claiming Jesus was the Messiah. However, according to his own account, at some point Paul received a revelation that changed his outlook (Gal. 3:12). From that point forward, he became an advocate not only of the new religion but of a specific form of Gentile (non-Jewish) Christianity. He taught that

Paul's First Journey and his Journey to Rome

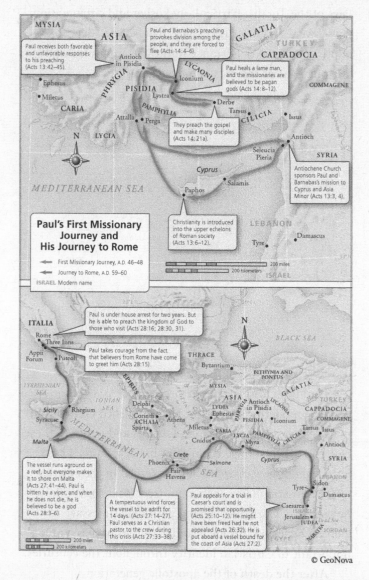

Paul's First Missionary Journey and His Journey to Rome

◄── First Missionary Journey, A.D. 46–48
◄── Journey to Rome, A.D. 59–60

ISRAEL Modern name

Paul receives both favorable and unfavorable responses to his preaching (Acts 13:42–45).

Paul and Barnabas's preaching provokes division among the people, and they are forced to flee (Acts 14:4–6).

Paul heals a lame man, and the missionaries are believed to be pagan gods (Acts 14:8–12).

They preach the gospel and make many disciples (Acts 14:21a).

Antiochene Church sponsors Paul and Barnabas's mission to Cyprus and Asia Minor (Acts 13:3, 4).

Christianity is introduced into the upper echelons of Roman society (Acts 13:6–12).

Paul is under house arrest for two years. But he is able to preach the kingdom of God to those who visit (Acts 28:16; 28:30, 31).

Paul takes courage from the fact that believers from Rome have come to greet him (Acts 28:15).

The vessel runs aground on a reef, but everyone makes it to shore on Malta (Acts 27:41–44). Paul is bitten by a viper, and when he does not die, he is believed to be a god (Acts 28:3–6)

A tempestuous wind forces the vessel to be adrift for 14 days. (Acts 27:14–27). Paul serves as a Christian pastor to the crew during this crisis (Acts 27:33–38).

Paul appeals for a trial in Caesar's court and is promised that opportunity (Acts 25:10–12). He might have been freed had he not appealed (Acts 26:32). He is put aboard a vessel bound for the coast of Asia (Acts 27:2).

© GeoNova

the life, death, and resurrection of Jesus meant that the laws of the Torah—particularly kosher and circumcision laws—were no longer necessary. Instead, he advocated baptism as a rite of entrance into the community, and faith in Jesus as the means for salvation.

Paul's Second and Third Journeys

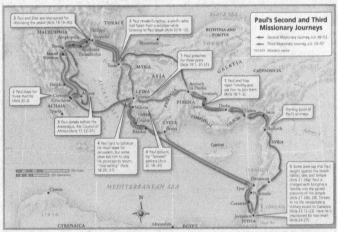

© GeoNova

Paul took his message to Greece and Asia Minor, which is modern-day Turkey. He established churches in many cities across the Roman Empire, and wrote to these churches to encourage them after his departure. These letters about new churches are preserved in the epistles of the Christian New Testament (see "Texts"). While not all early Christians agreed with Paul's message of Gentile inclusion, his ideas and activities have remained important to Christian identity throughout the centuries.

After the death of the apostolic generation, Christianity continued to spread throughout the Roman

Empire. Oftentimes, Christians encountered persecution because of their beliefs or because of rumors against them. Among the most famous of these rumors was that Christians were cannibals, since Christians called the wine "blood" and the bread "the body" during their communion ritual. Though the Roman Empire was responsible for much of the persecution against early Christians, the policy of Rome changed significantly when Galerius proclaimed an Edict of Toleration in 311 CE, and Constantine followed with the Edict of Milan in 313 CE. Under these edicts, Christianity became one of the officially sanctioned religions of the Empire. Christians were now allowed to meet openly and found it easier to establish hierarchies of church leadership, such as area bishops. Constantine also approved the convening of a council in 325 CE to establish official Christian beliefs. The Council of Nicea was the first of many throughout the centuries to discuss specific aspects of Christian belief, especially the nature of the Trinity (see "Beliefs").

The councils were one aspect of a movement in Christianity toward orthodoxy, establishing a single set of accepted beliefs. While early Christianity was a diverse tradition—there were Christians who kept Torah, others who rejected Torah completely, still others who were influenced by Greek philosophy, and so on—over a few centuries, many of these early beliefs were declared unorthodox. Officials of the church informed their parishioners which gospels were authoritative, and told their opponents why their beliefs were heretical. One prominent defender of orthodoxy was Augustine (354–430 CE), a bishop who famously framed the concepts of just war and original sin. He also wrote many lengthy treatises against beliefs he deemed to be heretical, including Manichaeism—a religion which combined Zoroastrian and Christian beliefs, and which he had practiced before converting to Christianity. Another notable guardian of orthodoxy is Athanasius, also a bishop, who is famous for defending his opposition to Arianism, the belief that Christ is subordinate to God the Father, and for offering the first list of all twenty-seven canonical New Testament books as part of an Easter letter to his parishioners in 367 CE.

Over the next few centuries, Christianity continued to grow. As it moved both east and west along the Mediterranean basin, especially after the fall of the Roman Empire, local communities developed very different beliefs and traditions. In the East, priests were allowed to marry, Greek was the dominant language, and two-dimensional paintings of Jesus or the saints, called icons, were venerated. In the West, priests remained celibate, Latin was the preferred language, and icons were considered to be idolatrous. These Christians also began to view the Bishop of Rome, the Pope, as the sole authority over all Christians; Christians in the East, however, viewed the Pope as one bishop among many who lived throughout the Mediterranean, and tended to favor the Bishop of Constantinople. Western Christians also added the phrase "and the Son" (in Latin, filioque) to the Nicene Creed's description of the role of the Holy Spirit and how it proceeds from God the Father in the Trinity. Eastern Christians, however, did not endorse this theological change to the common creed.

Inevitably, these differences caused a rift. In 1054 CE, the Pope and the Bishop of Constantinople, known as the Patriarch, excommunicated each other. Excommunication is removing someone from the ritual and sacramental life of the church, essentially condemning them until and unless the excommunicated person formally repents. Following this mutual excommunication, the church was split into two divisions: Orthodox and Roman Catholic. This was the first major split in Christianity, though not the only one (see "Divisions").

Around this same time, the division which was later called Roman Catholicism initially embarked upon the Crusades, which lasted almost 200 years, in response to the Islamic presence in Jerusalem. Pope Urban II, who famously called for the first Crusade during a sermon at Clermont, France, justified an armed attack to defend Jerusalem's freedom (see Asbridge). In reality, however, the Crusades were a brutal series of religious attacks across Europe. Even fellow Christians were not safe; in 1204 CE, when Crusaders came to the Orthodox stronghold of Constantinople, they desecrated the altar and destroyed the icons in the Hagia Sophia Orthodox church, even going so far as to place prostitutes on the holy seat of the Patriarch. Many thousands of Jews, Muslims, and Christians—including many who were not fighters—died during the Crusades, and the original task of retaking Jerusalem from Muslim Turks was never achieved.

In spite of the failure of the Crusades, Catholicism continued to solidify its power in Europe. By the eve of the Reformation, Catholicism was a force that exceeded many European governments, and the Pope was the

authority in both spiritual and state affairs. Among
the displays of this power were massive European
building projects funded by indulgences, fees paid to
delay punishment for sins which had been confessed
and absolved. At the time of the Reformation, the sale
of indulgences was notoriously abused and used to
manipulate ordinary people who feared the power of the
Church. One person who challenged this practice was
a German monk named Martin Luther, the eventual
founder of Protestantism.

Protestantism

Luther believed that indulgences were both
corrupt and theologically incorrect. He drew upon an
interpretation of the book of Romans, describing an
unmediated relationship between God and humanity
based only on faith, thus rendering indulgences
unnecessary. To promote his ideas, Luther posted *The
Ninety-Five Theses*, or belief statements, on the door of the
church in Wittenberg, Germany in 1517. In his twenty-
first statement, Luther writes, "Therefore those preachers
of indulgences are in error, who say that by the pope's
indulgences a man is freed from every penalty, and
saved; . . . [for the indulgences], gain and avarice can be
increased, but the result of the intercession of the Church
is in the power of God alone."

Luther's act of rebellion against the Catholic Church
resulted in him being forced to flee his home and seek
refuge among the principates of Germany. Eventually,
he was asked to defend his rebellious actions at the Diet

of Worms; a diet is a council which determines guilt or innocence in church matters.

Luther's demands for reform were both religious and political. The Catholic Church at the time claimed far-reaching political influence, and a rebellion against church doctrine was a rebellion against civil order. Indeed, as Germany adopted Lutheranism, it moved away from the Catholic political structure and toward autonomous statehood. Additionally, as the new protest movement grew, other countries also moved away from Catholic influence in civil affairs.

A second major Protestant reformer was John Calvin, who founded the denominations collectively known as Reformed Christianity. Calvin's major dispute with the Catholic Church was also related to the belief that one could purchase salvation, though Calvin answered this question differently from Martin Luther. Instead of suggesting that salvation was a free gift from God's abundant love, Calvin believed that salvation was predestined, or completely predetermined from the beginning of time for all humanity.

Calvin described predestination in his famous work *The Institutes of Christian Religion*. Using scriptural support and an appeal to logic, Calvin claimed that for all people, God had already determined whether they were destined for eternal bliss in heaven or eternal damnation in hell. He argued that if it were up to humans to determine their eternal state, then God would not be all-knowing—since humans would have the freedom to make a real, independent choice—nor would grace be God's free gift, since it would have to be equally available to all.

Furthermore, the biblical text is full of examples of God choosing some people, like the Hebrews, and not others, or favoring certain individuals over others, like Jacob over Esau. To Calvin, this was irrefutable proof that God had already determined who would be saved or condemned. Calvin believed that Christians, whom he called the elect, should live out their days without worrying about their eternal states. Calvin was most active in Switzerland, where he set up communities dedicated to these principles, and his beliefs went on to influence Presbyterianism and Dutch Reformism in Europe and the United States.

Anglicanism is a third major denomination that came out of the Protestant Reformation, although its founding was more explicitly political than that of Lutheranism or Calvinism. As previously noted, the Catholic Church exercised significant power in both religious and political affairs. In England, this meant that the king was obligated to the Pope, and as a result, the king was expected to marry a wife who would be advantageous to the Catholic power structure. In the case of King Henry VIII, he was required to marry Catherine of Aragon, a member of the Spanish royalty. This marriage would solidify the relations between England and Spain, both of which were loyal to the Pope. However, Henry rejected Catherine, claiming that she was unable to bear a male heir to the throne. He wished to annul his marriage to her, but this was unacceptable under Catholic law.

To solve this problem, Henry declared himself the head of a new church, the Church of England. In his position as sole and final authority of this new church,

Henry declared his marriage to Catherine invalid and married Anne Boleyn instead. Henry also went on to marry four other women over his reign. The church he founded struggled to continue, most notably during the reign of Mary Tudor, who reverted the English state religion to Catholicism. Eventually, however, the Church of England established its reformed Anglican identity by means of the *Thirty-Nine Articles*, written during the reign of Queen Elizabeth I in 1563.

Luther, Calvin, and Henry all tried to correct perceived abuses of power in the Church, but theirs were not the only attempts at reform. Catholics also made attempts to reform from within and sought to respond to Protestant charges in several ways. Some reforms came from grass-roots movements, even before the outside protests. For example, to address the perception that Catholic clergy were overly secular because of their engagement in politics, new monastic orders like the Theatines were founded with the goal of improving clergy spiritual formation. The Capuchin order ministered among the poor and sick, attempting to live in the most austere manner possible, in contrast to the massive wealth of the Vatican. Additionally, the Ursuline order was founded in Italy to educate children, particularly young girls, so that they might read the Scriptures for themselves. These monastic reforms were astoundingly successful, but they were not immediately validated by Church leadership. During most of the Reformation period, the official papal position was articulated by the Council of Trent (1545–63), which vehemently opposed the ideas of Protestant dissenters. In contrast, the Council reaffirmed the belief in transubstantiation, the authority of the Pope, and the importance of works as well as faith for salvation, denying the essential arguments of Protestant reformers.

As a part of its counter-Reformation plan, the Catholic Church also attempted to reclaim a spiritual foothold among territories lost to Protestantism. Founded by Ignatius of Loyola in 1540, the Jesuits, or Society of Jesus, were pivotal to this endeavor. Ignatius envisioned a new order of monks, governed by the strict standards of his own writings called *Spiritual Exercises*, in which members saw themselves as missionaries, warriors, and monks. The Jesuits were fervent defenders of the Pope. They spread throughout Europe with hopes of reconverting heretical Protestants, and then continued on to Asia. The Jesuits were successful in stemming the tide of Protestantism in Europe, particularly in France and the Netherlands.

Over the next several centuries, Christianity was again transformed, this time by its spread to Africa, the Americas, and East Asia by means of Spanish conquistadors and dissident groups from the Church of England, including the Puritans and the Quakers.

In recent times, Christianity has also struggled with the challenge of modernity. With the rise of scientific thinking and equality movements like feminism, Christians have been forced to address how they relate to people who are at odds with the ancient beliefs of the church. Some Christian groups have embraced modernity, but others have rejected modern ideals in favor of more literal readings of the Bible. For example, fundamentalists have rejected evolutionary theory and have promoted the literal truth of the Genesis creation narrative, and some fundamentalists have also favored more submissive roles for women, mirroring those in the Bible, in contrast to the principles described in the Equal Rights Amendment.

There are now more than two billion Christians worldwide. While Christianity is diminishing in numbers across Europe, Christian populations continue to grow in parts of South America, Africa, and Asia.

DIVISIONS

Three main divisions exist within Christianity: Roman Catholicism, Eastern Orthodoxy, and Protestantism. From these three main groups, many smaller splinter groups also arose. Roman Catholicism and Eastern Orthodoxy grew out of the split between Christians in the East and West during the eleventh century (see "From Judaism to Christianity"). Then Protestantism arose during the Reformation, initiated by Martin Luther in 1517 (see "Protestantism").

Today, Roman Catholicism is the largest single division in Christianity. Throughout the centuries, Catholicism spread across the world as European nations conquered other lands. Countries that were predominantly Catholic, like France and Spain, took religion along with them as they conquered other peoples, often forcibly imposing it on the preexisting population. For this reason, Catholic Christianity is now the largest religious group in South and Central America, the United States, the Philippines, and some parts of sub-Saharan Africa

(see https://www.cia.gov/library/publications/the-world
-factbook/fields/2122.html).

Catholic Christians maintain several unique beliefs
and practices which distinguish them from other types of
Christians. For example, Catholics view the Pope as the
sole authority over all Christians, and they believe that
the statements he makes *ex cathedra*—from the seat of
papal authority—are infallible. Catholicism also maintains
a celibate, unmarried, male priesthood, and incorporates
the existence of purgatory, a realm in the afterlife where
sins may be cleansed so that a person might eventually
enter heaven. Transubstantiation, or the belief that the
bread and wine of the Eucharist mystically become the
body and blood of Christ, is also specific to Catholicism.
While the Catholic Church used to mandate that Mass be
celebrated in Latin only, contemporary Catholic practice
allows for Mass in the common language, or vernacular, of
the congregation.

The second largest group of Christians worldwide
is collectively known as Orthodox; though some people
describe this group as "Eastern Orthodox," simply
"Orthodox" is the more preferred term. Orthodox
Christianity is actually composed of several smaller
groups, usually identified by language or geographical
area: Greek Orthodox, Russian Orthodox, Armenian
Orthodox, and Egyptian Orthodox (Coptic) are all
examples.

In Orthodox Christianity, worship typically includes
the use of icons, which are paintings of Jesus or the saints.
These paintings are created according to exact standards
for both the images and the materials. Usually placing

these icons in churches or homes, Orthodox Christians often pray and light candles in front of them. Non-Orthodox Christians sometimes misunderstand the role of icons in Orthodox worship, confusing these veneration practices with idol worship. However, icons serve as aids in worshipping God, not the actual objects of worship. Just as a non-Orthodox Christian might light a candle to improve focus before offering a prayer, an Orthodox Christian might use an icon as a sort of window through which a person may better see the mystery of God. Icons also serve as visual reminders of Scripture and the lives of the saints, both of which serve as ethical models for the believer.

Orthodox Christians also have a unique organizational structure, being composed of several self-governing groups, whereas the Catholic Church is a single entity, united under the singular authority of the Pope. Though Orthodox Christians give the Patriarch of Constantinople a great deal of respect, he does not have the same level of authority as the Pope. In addition, whereas Catholic priests must remain unmarried and celibate, Orthodox priests are allowed to marry while serving congregations. However, Orthodox bishops are expected to remain celibate.

Protestantism is the third major Christian division, having origins in sixteenth-century protest movements against perceived abuses by the Catholic Church. Protestants reject the centralized authority of the Pope as well as the belief that an intermediary like a priest is needed to interpret Scripture or offer reconciliation. Protestantism had an early emphasis on decentralization and autonomy, and as a result, Protestant beliefs vary widely.

In spite of this diversity of beliefs, Protestants share an enhanced emphasis on Scripture over church leadership or sacrament as the means through which to encounter God. Protestants contend that all believers are priests and are capable of understanding and interpreting Scripture. Martin Luther called this concept *Sola Scriptura*, or "Scripture Alone." For this reason, most Protestant churches emphasize preaching based on biblical passages in their worship services.

Today, Protestantism is constituted of many denominations, most of which stem from the protest movements of Martin Luther or John Calvin, or the rebellion of the Church of England. Lutheranism is the dominant form of Christianity in Germany, Finland, Denmark, and Sweden; it is also widespread in the United States, particularly in areas where immigrants from these nations came to reside. Lutherans are also the majority Christian group in Namibia. Calvinist groups include the various Reformed congregations, including Presbyterianism and the Dutch Reformed churches. Calvinism is popular in Holland and Scotland, and today there are also large Reformed communities in Iowa and Michigan. The Church of England is still the official state church in Great Britain, and Anglicanism has spawned several denominations of its own, including Episcopalianism and Methodism. New Zealand, Australia, Nigeria, and Uganda also have significant Anglican populations.

While Lutheranism, Calvinism, and Anglicanism make up the largest Protestant denominations, the diversity of modern Protestantism extends far beyond these three groups. For example, some Protestants come from "free spirit" movements of the Reformation, including the Unitarians, who reject Trinitarianism. Others come from the Anabaptist reforms, which also have origins in the Reformation. Anabaptists (literally, "re-baptizers") claimed that only adult baptism was true baptism; thus, those baptized as infants must be re-baptized. Mennonites, Amish Christians, and members of the Church of the Brethren continued this tradition in the United States. Interestingly, the scholarly consensus is that modern-day Baptist denominations do not trace their history to the Anabaptists, but to a separatist movement that splintered from the Church of England. Baptist churches in America were heavily influenced by the revivalism movements of the eighteenth and nineteenth centuries, and are still marked by a charismatic orientation.

BELIEFS

Though it is difficult to pinpoint any universal Christian beliefs, there are a few key ideas which are widespread across many Christian groups, including belief in the Trinity, the sacredness of Scripture, and a linear view of time.

The Trinity is the Christian concept that God is one deity in three persons, usually named as Father, Son, and Holy Spirit. While the word "trinity" is nowhere in the Bible, within a few centuries of the death of Jesus,

Trinitarianism was a defining feature of Christian belief, primarily because a series of church councils met specifically to discuss the Trinity. Early in Christian history, believers were faced with a key question: Who is Jesus? Jewish messianism emphasized the military and political role of the "anointed one," but did not claim that the coming Messiah was divine, since this would be an affront to monotheism (for more on Jewish monotheism, see "Beliefs" in the section on Judaism in this book). However, Jesus was not a military or political savior, as had been expected; in fact, he suffered a humiliating defeat at the hands of Rome. Christians began to view Jesus not as a political liberator, but as a spiritual one; his "humiliating" death was actually an important part of his unique status as God's son, and was necessary to achieve human salvation.

Since early Christians drew from Jewish concepts of monotheism, but still wanted to claim a unique relationship between God and Jesus, they needed to explain the connection between Father and Son. Was Jesus a true child, whom God had procreated, or was the Christ eternally an aspect of God? How did the human Jesus contain divinity—that is, God's "substance?" And how did both Father and Son relate to a third biblical concept, The Holy Spirit, as described in Matthew, John, and the Pauline epistles? It was these questions that the series of ecumenical councils sought to answer. While an outsider may consider these matters to be of minimal importance, for Christians they were critical to establishing orthodoxy and avoiding beliefs that might lead to damnation. From this series of very intense and occasionally angry discussions came several statements of orthodox Christian belief, known as creeds.

The first ecumenical council to discuss this issue was held in Nicea, in modern-day Turkey. In 325 CE, bishops met to begin constructing the Nicene Creed, which is still used in churches today. It describes the relationship between Father, Son, and Holy Spirit as, "One God, the Father Almighty . . . and one Lord, Jesus Christ, the son of God, the only-begotten of the Father, that is of the substance of the Father, God from God, light from light, true God from true God, begotten not made . . . and in the Holy Ghost, the Lord and Giver of life, who proceeds from the Father, who with the Father and the Son together is worshiped and glorified." The concept of the Trinity continues to be a formative belief for most Christians, with the notable exception of Unitarians.

A second common conviction among Christians is the authority of Scripture. Christians generally consider the Bible to be the inspired word of God, though what this means varies widely across traditions. For some, inspiration refers to God's relationship with humans being the source of the Scriptures; these Christians affirm that human beings wrote the Bible, and that human error is possible in its pages. On the other extreme, some Christians contend that inspiration means that God wrote each word of the text using the hand of a human writer, and that the resultant text is therefore devoid of human error. This idea is known as inerrancy, and is commonly held among fundamentalist forms of Christianity. Regardless of their positions on the authorship of

Scripture, most Christians see the Bible as a source of guidance and assurance in their day-to-day lives.

Finally, like their Abrahamic counterparts, Christians largely believe time to be a linear phenomenon. This makes Christianity different from traditions like Hinduism and Buddhism, in which people view the world as endlessly regenerating. For Christians, each person lives only one time, and at death (or on a future day of resurrection), he or she will face individual judgment. Similarly, Christians believe the world came into existence at one point in history and will end someday in the future. This belief is most pronounced in apocalyptic Christian movements, which consider the descriptions in the Apocalypse of John, also called Revelation, to be a literal description of God's judgment at the end of time.

Sacred Texts

Not only was Christianity born from Jewish ideas of messianism and apocalypticism, but the early Christians drew their first scriptures from Judaism as well. The Hebrew Bible, which Christians eventually called the Old Testament, contains Jewish origins, laws, promises, and prophecies. Most early Christians saw the Hebrew Bible as connected to and fulfilled by the life of Jesus. Both Paul and the author of the Gospel of Matthew, for example, often quote Hebrew scriptures to support their claims that Jesus is a unique fulfillment of God's promises. These scriptures became the first part of the Christian canon.

Along with the Hebrew Bible, early Christians also gave authority to additional writings. The first writings to gain prominence were the epistles of Paul, which were letters written to Paul's various churches and which were eventually circulated more widely throughout the Mediterranean. These letters were occasional, meaning that they were prompted by certain events in the churches to which Paul felt he needed to respond, and they vary widely in tone and length.

Paul writes often about the way Jesus's life, death, and resurrection make possible a new relationship between God and all people, including Gentiles, or non-Jews. This new relationship is not because of any deserving human actions, according to Paul, but instead depends on God acting in love through Jesus, and then humans receiving that gift graciously—an act he calls justification "by faith apart from works prescribed by the law" (Romans 3:28). Because this justification requires no human action, which Paul calls "works," anyone can be reconciled to God. Paul thus emphasizes, "There is neither Jew nor Greek, male nor female, slave nor free, but all are one in Christ Jesus" (Gal. 3:28).

However, Paul's epistles were not the only letters being circulated among early Christians. Other apostles wrote to their churches, too. These epistles sometimes clashed with Paul's assessments. The writer of the Epistle of James, for example, claimed that "faith by itself, if it has no works, is dead" (2:17), a sentiment with which Paul would have certainly disagreed. The author of the Epistles of Peter proclaims that a person should "address as Father the one who judges impartially according to each one's works" (1 Peter 1:17).

In another group of letters often called the Pastoral Epistles, some scholars doubt Pauline authorship. Those scholars instead believe that authors claimed Pauline authority at least a generation after Paul's death. For scholars pseudonymity would allow believers to adapt Paul's ideas to their new situation with a more complex church structure. The church accepted these letters as written by Paul, but other letters were rejected as heretical. A total of twenty-one epistles are a part of the Christian canon.

Along with these letters, the Christian church eventually canonized four gospels. The gospels were not composed when Jesus was alive, and they certainly do not predate the authentic letters of Paul. Scholars believe that the earliest of the canonical gospels is Mark, which was likely written around 70 CE, nearly forty years after Jesus's death. The Gospels of Matthew and Luke were written a decade later, and the Gospel of John was completed another decade after that.

The gospels are not intended to be day-to-day records of Jesus's every word and deed. Focused on the good news of the "kingdom of God," which Jesus preached was coming on earth, the gospel writers make no claim that every event in his life was equally important. Indeed, large periods of Jesus's life are not mentioned at all. Instead, the gospel writers focus almost exclusively on three types of material related to Jesus's life: sayings, miracle stories, and passion (suffering and death) narratives.

Among the most well-known of Jesus's sayings are parables. Parables are short stories, often in an agrarian setting, that use metaphor to describe the "kingdom of God" about which Jesus so frequently preached. The meaning behind the parables is not always clear. They are not allegories, in which every item in the story represents something in the real world. Instead, the parables are word-pictures, meant to evoke feelings and images rather than a straightforward equation of ideas. Even with this ambiguity, images from parables have persisted and have become part of our common vocabulary; the phrases "good Samaritan," "lost sheep," "prodigal son," and "pearls before swine" all come from parable sources.

Both nature miracles and healing miracle stories are common in the gospels. The nature miracles include stories of Jesus stilling storms (Mark 4:35–41), turning water into wine (John 2:1–11), and cursing a fig tree until it withers (Matt. 21:18–22). Healing miracles include restoring a paralyzed man (Luke 5:18–19), healing a hemorrhaging woman (Mark 5:24–29), and raising Lazarus from death to life (John 11:1–46). The healing and nature miracles are intended to point to the compassion of God for the least in society as well as God's power over the forces of chaos. For first-century Christians, these stories would have affirmed Jesus as a chosen one of God, a messiah.

While sayings and miracle stories are key components of each gospel, the gospel writers emphasize the passion of Jesus above all else. These stories are the most detailed in the gospels; almost each moment from the Passover meal to the burial is vividly described. While they differ in many details, the four canonical gospel writers all emphasize a shared Passover meal to which Jesus ascribes new meaning, Jesus's betrayal by his disciple Judas, and the physical suffering and death of Jesus on a cross. The gospel writers note that after Jesus's execution and the Sabbath day of rest, some female disciples visit the tomb to anoint Jesus's body and find the tomb empty. The message of Jesus's resurrection in the canonical gospels is the culmination of the passion narratives and the central *euangelion* of the early church.

A third category of New Testament literature is apocalyptic in nature. There is only one full-length apocalypse in the canon, the Apocalypse of John, which is the last book in the Christian New Testament. People generally write apocalyptic literature during times of intense persecution, and they use veiled language and imagery to communicate to the oppressed about a coming day of liberation. Coded language is necessary to protect the community from further persecution. For example, John uses the term *Babylon*, a very old empire that once destroyed Jerusalem and then itself was eventually destroyed, to refer to the coming destruction of the Roman Empire. Coded language like this would make sense to John's audience, and would give them comfort in times of distress, but would also keep potential persecutors from seeing the true message. As much later readers, modern Christians sometimes misunderstand the meaning and purpose of apocalyptic imagery, leading to end-of-the-world predictions which fail to materialize.

The gospels (including the two-part Luke-Acts), epistles, and Apocalypse of John make up the entire Christian New Testament. Along with the Hebrew Bible, these books form the common canon of all Christians. During the Reformation, Protestants rejected fourteen additional books which had been included in the Old Testament until that time. These books are known collectively as the Apocrypha, or deuterocanonical books.

Rites and Rituals

As with sacred writings, rites and rituals among Christians vary depending on denomination. Orthodox Christians and Roman Catholics identify seven sacred rites and rituals, called sacraments; most Protestants identify two, and some recognize no rites or rituals at all.

For most Christians, entrance into the faith community is marked by baptism, a ritual washing with water. Baptism is rooted in biblical practices, especially Jesus's own baptism in the Jordan River (Mark 1:9–13) and the recommendation of baptism as an alternative to circumcision for Gentiles (Col. 2:11–13). Modern Christian baptismal practice varies widely, both in terms of age and method. Most Christians practice infant baptism, but some believe that consent of the baptized is necessary and practice only adult baptism. While some Christians fully immerse the baptized person, many others use poured or sprinkled water. Most Christians do agree, however, that baptism is a once-in-a-lifetime event. Baptism is practiced by all Christian denominations.

For Catholic and Orthodox Christians, another sacrament is Confirmation, which is the act of personally accepting the vows of church membership taken by one's parents at baptism. Since these churches practice infant baptism, confirmation allows a young adult to independently confirm the basic beliefs of the church community. Confirmation often involves preparatory classes at the young adult's church, and is sometimes paired with First Communion.

Communion—also called Eucharist, the Lord's Supper, or Mass—is another common Christian sacrament. This sacrament is a ritual remembrance of Jesus's last supper with his disciples, at the Passover, before his betrayal and crucifixion. Today, Christians remember this meal by consuming bread and wine (or, in some churches, juice) as a community, usually during a worship service. While the practice of communion is common to most Christians, the associated meaning varies widely depending on denomination. Roman Catholics and some Orthodox Christians, for example, believe that the elements of communion are transformed into the true body and blood of Christ at the moment the priest elevates them, a process called transubstantiation. Lutheran Protestants claim instead that the bread and wine remains bread and wine while at the same time holding the body of Christ, an idea called consubstantiation. Still other groups, including Baptists, believe that the bread and wine are purely symbolic and do not change.

Marriage is considered a sacred rite by most Christians, and is seen as the fourth of seven sacraments in the Orthodox and Catholic Churches. Christian marriage usually involves the blessing of a clergy person and an exchange of vows and rings, though practices vary widely depending on local customs and culture.

The Sacrament of Penance, often called reconciliation or confession, is a fifth sacrament in non-Protestant churches. Reconciliation is the process of admitting one's sins to a priest, who offers absolution to the individual. In Catholic churches, reconciliation often takes place in confessionals, which are small booths to the side of the main sanctuary. These booths allow the priest and confessor to hear one another without being face-to-face. In the United States, sins confessed to a priest are considered protected communication and cannot be used against that person in a court of law.

A sixth sacrament in Orthodox and Catholic traditions is that of Holy Orders, which include bishops, deacons, priests, monks, and nuns. Ordination is the process by which these holy orders are conferred upon a candidate or initiate, a person who has chosen a lifelong commitment to church service and who takes vows expressing that commitment. In the Roman Catholic Church, poverty, obedience, and celibacy are requirements for those taking Holy Orders. Eastern Orthodox ordinates share these vows, though priests can be ordained if they are already married. If they are currently unmarried or widowed, however, they must not marry after ordination. Protestants do not consider the Holy Orders a sacrament, but they do ordain pastors, bishops, and deacons. In Protestant churches, celibacy is not required of the ordained, and some churches have expanded ordination rites to include traditionally under-represented groups, such as women and homosexuals.

The final sacrament is variously known as the Anointing of the Sick, Holy Unction, or Last Rites. In Orthodox churches, anointing with oil is available to ill people, even if they are not near death. In Catholicism, though one need not be on the point of death to receive the sacrament, the Vatican reserves this ritual for those "in danger of death from sickness or old age," according to the *Catechism of the Catholic Church*. The Anointing of the Sick is an opportunity for the ill or dying person to prepare for death. The priest performing last rites will hear the confession of the dying person and absolve these sins, and then the priest will often offer the Eucharist as a reminder of the resurrection; this final Eucharist is called *viaticum*.

Along with these sacramental rites, most Christians share a series of holy days throughout the year. The most important are in the spring, beginning with Ash Wednesday and continuing through Lent, a forty-day period of preparation concluding with the celebration of Easter. Lent is often marked by fasting, prayer, and acts of mercy among Christians who keep this season. Lent commemorates the last days of Jesus's life and culminates in Holy Week. Holy Week begins with Palm Sunday, remembering Jesus's lauded entry into Jerusalem before his betrayal. The following Thursday is known as Maundy Thursday, from the Latin word *maundatum*, meaning commandment, which remembers Jesus's last supper with his disciples and his commandment to "love one another" (John 13:34–35). The next day is remembered as Good Friday, recalling the day of the crucifixion, and is followed by Easter, the Sunday celebration of the resurrection. Eastern Orthodox Christians use a different calendar to calculate the date of Easter than Roman Catholic and Protestant Christians, and all traditions have a moveable date for the holiday based on the time of the full moon after the Spring equinox. Fifty days after Easter, Christians celebrate Pentecost, recalling when God sent the Holy Spirit to form the Christian Church (Acts 2:1–4).

A second holy season occurs in late fall and early winter, comprised of the four Sundays of Advent leading to Christmas, and continuing to Epiphany. Advent is considered a time of preparation for Christmas, as Lent is for Easter, but is generally regarded as a more festive time; for example, no fasting is required during Advent like it is during Lent. Sundays in Advent are usually marked with the lighting of four candles to mark the passing weeks; this candle lighting culminates with a Christmas Eve service in which the Christ candle is lit, and the birth of Jesus is commemorated as "the light of the world" (John 8:12). Many Christians also illuminate their homes and evergreen trees to celebrate the season. The date for Christmas is another that varies based on denomination; Protestants and Catholics celebrate on December 25 according to the Gregorian calendar; Greek Orthodox Christians celebrate Christmas according to the older Julian calendar, which results in a January 7 date for Christmas; and Armenian Orthodox Christians celebrate Christmas on January 19. Twelve days called Christmastide follow the celebration of Christmas leading to Epiphany, which means "manifestation." During Epiphany, Christians remember the coming of the wise men as told in Matthew 2:1–12, as well as other miracles in which God's power was manifested through Jesus.

Some Christians do not celebrate the rites, rituals, or holidays above. Christian diversity yields sacred practices as widely divergent as Christian belief. For example, Jehovah's Witnesses do not celebrate Easter or Christmas, and they offer the Lord's Supper, which they call the Memorial, only once a year. As another example,

Protestants do not believe in the Sacrament of Penance, instead believing that forgiveness must be asked directly of God, not through a priestly intermediary. This diversity ought not lead anyone to believe that some Christians are "more authentic" than others; instead, it simply indicates the ways the very ancient message of Jesus has been appropriated to be meaningful to a wide variety of believers.

FOR FURTHER READING

Asbridge, Thomas. *The First Crusade: A New History*. Oxford University Press: Oxford, 2005.

Browning, W.R.F., ed. *A Dictionary of the Bible*. Oxford: Oxford University Press, 1996.

Coogan, Michael, et al. *The New Oxford Annotated Bible with Apocrypha*. Oxford: Oxford University Press, 2010.

Ferguson, Everett. *Backgrounds of Early Christianity*. Eerdmans: Grand Rapids, 2003.

MacCollough, Diarmaid. *Christianity: The First Three Thousand Years*. New York: Penguin, 2010.

Nichols, Stephen J. *The Reformation: How a Monk and a Mallet Changed the World*. Wheaton, IL: Crossway, 2007.

Payton, James R. *Light from the Christian East: An Introduction to the Orthodox Tradition*. Downers Grove, IL: Intervarsity Press, 2007.

*Man praying
in mosque*

ISLAM

INTRODUCTION

Islam has many features in common with Judaism and Christianity. These three religions share the same God, similar prophets, and the same linear view of human history with a beginning, middle, and ultimate day of judgment. The three also share Abraham as a common ancestor, and therefore are often called Abrahamic religions. Some people call Muslims, Jews, and Christians "People of the Book" because they believe all three religions have scriptures revealed by God. However, in spite of their commonalities, many Jews and Christians misunderstand Islam. This chapter will provide a better understanding of Islamic beliefs and practices, while at the same time correcting misconceptions commonly held by non-Muslims.

HISTORY

In the sixth century CE, the city of Mecca on the Arabian Peninsula was a bustling center of trade and religion. Inside the city was a very old stone, possibly a meteorite, which had become a pilgrimage site dedicated to local deities. Though the common religion in Arabia was polytheistic, this pilgrimage site was also known to Jews and Christians. Religious pilgrims brought economic prosperity and abundant trade to Mecca. Muhammad was born into this religious diversity at around 570 CE.

Muhammad's early life was difficult. His parents died while he was still young, leaving him orphaned and illiterate. He was raised by an uncle but never received any formal education. When he was in his twenties, he worked with a caravan company and fell in love with Khadija, the caravan owner and a distant cousin of Muhammad. They married when he was twenty-five, and she was forty. Together they had two sons and four daughters.

As he grew older, Muhammad began meditating in mountain caves outside Mecca. Through his travels with the caravan, Muhammad had encountered Judaism, Christianity, and probably Zoroastrianism, all of which share a belief in one god, or Allah in Arabic. Muhammad had also experienced the religious diversity of Mecca, but he believed that the worship of many gods favored by most of his people was idolatrous. According to Islamic tradition, in 611 CE, Muhammad was in contemplation about these religious matters when he received a revelation. The angel Gabriel, to whom Muslims refer as Jibril, appeared to him saying, "Recite!" Muhammad, though uneducated, submitted to God's command. He remembered and recited Jibril's words, which were sent from God, and this act of submission gave the world the Qur'an (see "Sacred Texts").

The revelations to Muhammad happened over a period of several years, but the message he received was always consistent: God is one, and all people should submit to God's will. The religion which eventually developed from these revelations is called Islam, which means "submission." One who submits to God's will is therefore known as a Muslim.

Muhammad's submission to God had immediate and important consequences. First, the revelations to Muhammad were collected and became the Qur'an, which was completed and closed within a generation of Muhammad's lifetime. Furthermore, as Jibril had commanded, Muhammad went into the city of Mecca proclaiming the oneness of God, a belief known as monotheism (see "Major Beliefs"). However, polytheism was deeply ingrained in the surrounding culture, so Muhammad's proclamations were not well received, and the few people who converted were heavily persecuted. Eventually, Muhammad and the small band of converts were forced to flee to nearby Yathrib, later renamed Medina, to avoid persecution. This event in 622 CE is known as the Hijra, or migration, and Muslim calendars are dated from this year. For example, 2011 on the common calendar is year 1432 AH, after the Hijrah.

In Yathrib, Muhammad's situation improved, though it was not perfect. The Prophet was given some political authority, and Muslims were recognized as one of the city's tribes. However, a charter was created to protect other religions in the city, including Christianity and Judaism. Muhammad was particularly in conflict with the Jewish population of Yathrib, and it was during this time that Muhammad began encouraging his believers to pray facing Mecca instead of Jerusalem. In Yathrib, the number of Muslim converts grew rapidly, and by 630 CE, Muhammad returned to Mecca along with 10,000 Muslim followers to take the city and rededicate the sanctuary of the sacred stone, called the Ka'aba, to Allah. From that date forward, Mecca became a Muslim city and remains so to this day; presently, Saudi law prohibits non-Muslims from entering the holy city.

Muhammad only lived for two more years after his victory in Mecca. He died in 632 CE. At his funeral, his good friend abu-Bakr stated, "If anyone worships Muhammad, Muhammad is dead, but if anyone worships Allah, he is alive and dies not." The words of abu-Bakr serve to remind us that even at this early date in the history of Islam, Muhammad was not regarded as a deity to be worshipped. From his first revelation until his death, people understood Muhammad to be fully human. Muslims believe that his submission made the revelation of the Qur'an possible, which is a miracle and blessing, but Muhammad himself was not perfect. Instead, Muslims call Muhammad "The Prophet," often with the designation PBUH, which means "Peace Be Upon Him."

After Muhammad's death, Muhammad had no male heir to become his successor; though Muhammad had a number of children during his lifetime, only a single daughter Fatima outlived him. As a result, conflict arose over how the new leader should be chosen. One side argued that future leaders should be chosen by the community and need not be biologically related to the Prophet. The other side contended that leadership should remain within Muhammad's family. This difference of opinion created a rift, worsened by the suspicious death of Ali, Muhammad's son-in-law and potential hereditary successor, in 661 CE. Ali's death, as well as the death of Ali's son Husayn at the battle of Karbala (modern Iraq) in 680 CE, solidified the division between these two groups. Today Islam remains in two major factions; the group advocating leadership chosen by the community is called Sunni, and the group promoting leadership from Muhammad's family is Shia, or Shi'ite, Islam (see "Major Divisions").

In spite of these internal divisions over leadership, Islam spread rapidly following Muhammad's death. By 711 CE, Islamic influence had spread as far west as Spain, though it was stopped from additional northward European expansion in 732 CE at the Battle of Tours. Muslim communities also moved into North Africa, Judea, and Persia. Over the next three hundred years, Islam began to spread into India and other parts of Asia. As Islam expanded geographically, Muslims developed both religious and political footholds in the countries they conquered, and often experienced conflict with their Christian neighbors. One of the greatest disputes was over the city of Jerusalem, which resulted in the centuries-long Crusades.

As Islam has entered the modern era, it has often struggled with the changes of modernity. Of particular concern is the perception of liberal attitudes in many non-Muslim nations. In predominantly Islamic areas, Westernization is often equated with loose morality, and steps have been taken to limit Western influence. Perhaps the most well-known example of this rejection is the Iranian revolution, which occurred in 1979. In that year, Iranians overthrew the Shah of Iran, who was supported by the United States, and installed the Ayatollah Khomeini as the head of government. Ayatollahs are primarily religious leaders (see "Major Divisions"), but in this case religious and governmental leadership were synonymous. Iran is a strong opponent of Westernization and remains an Islamic theocracy today. Islamic values have played a role in fighting Western influence in other countries as well. For example, in Africa at the beginning of the twentieth century, many countries were occupied by European powers and had been heavily missionized by European Christians. When the colonized Africans revolted against these occupying powers, many embraced Islam as a part of their independence as well.

Today Islam is the fastest growing religion in the world. It is the dominant religion in many nations throughout Africa and Asia, including Indonesia and Morocco, and in the United States, there are approximately 2.6 million Muslims.

MAJOR BELIEFS AND PRACTICES

The Five Pillars of Islam are the beliefs and rituals that make up the main practices of the religion.

Shahadah

The First Pillar of Islam is the profession of faith, called the Shahadah. Recitation of the Shahadah by at least two people in good faith is all that is necessary to be considered a Muslim. Believers incorporate the Shahadah into daily prayers, fathers whisper it to their babies at birth, and the faithful hope to have those words on their lips at the moment of death.

The two most important beliefs of Islam are summed up in the Shahadah, which states, "There is no god but Allah, and Muhammad is Allah's Prophet." Monotheism and the prophetic line, as summarized in this statement, constitute the core of Islam.

First and foremost, Islam is a monotheistic religion. Muslims believe in the oneness of God, and that this one God is separate from, while still in relationship with, humankind. God created the world, is sovereign over it, and will judge its inhabitants on the resurrection day. Above all, for devout Muslims:

> Allah is One.
> Allah is he on whom all depend.
> He begets not, nor is he begotten.
> And none is like him. (Surah 112)

As already mentioned, Muslims refer to God using the Arabic title Allah. Some non-Muslims think that this title indicates Muslims worship a different God than Jews or Christians, but this is not the case. In fact, Arabic-speaking Christians also refer to God as Allah.

The second part of the Shahadah states, "Muhammad is Allah's Prophet." Muhammad's designation as the Prophet (*rasul* in Arabic) does not mean that he was divine, since that would be opposed to the strict monotheism of Islam. It also does not mean that he was a prognosticator, as the popular understanding of the word "prophet" might suggest. Instead, it sets him as the last in a long line of people who spoke on behalf of God to humanity, including many figures recognizable to Jews and Christians: Noah, Abraham, Ishmael, Moses, John and Jesus, among others. Muslims contend that throughout the centuries, these prophets have proclaimed the oneness of God and the need for submission to God's

perfect will. The Qur'anic story of Noah is a good example
of this emphasis on proclamation. In the Jewish Torah
and Christian Old Testament, Noah does not speak at all
in the days preceding the flood. In the Qur'an, however,
Noah gives a lengthy speech beginning with the call to
submission: "O my people! Surely I am a plain warner
to you: that you should serve Allah and be careful of
(your duty to) Him." (Surah 71). Muslims believe that
the people did not properly receive Noah's message, that
the message was manipulated over time, or that it was
forgotten until the revelation to Muhammad, after which
no more revelations were needed. For this reason, Muslims
often refer to Muhammad as the "Seal of the Prophets,"
meaning that though many prophets have come before
him, no more will follow. Muhammad is the final and
greatest prophet in this succession.

Salat

The second pillar is Salat, or daily prayer. A devout
Muslim is required to pray five times a day—before
sunrise, noon, late afternoon, after sunset, and at night—
facing the holy city of Mecca. Believers are called to
prayer by a muezzin from a tall tower called a minaret in
Muslim communities. Salat incorporates specific actions
for the person praying. First, the believer washes hands,
arms, face, and feet; then he or she clears space for prayer,
often with a prayer rug. Next, the person faces Mecca and
stands, bows, and prostrates, which means kneeling on the
floor and touching one's head and hands to the ground.
Then he or she recites the prayers in Arabic, whether
or not the person understands the Arabic language.

Of course, not all prayer is as structured as Salat; spontaneous prayer may occur at other times. However, by such regulation, Salat is intended to create a feeling of unity with other believers, who are all saying the same words, facing the same direction, and positioning their bodies in the same manner at similar times throughout the day.

On Fridays, noon prayers are often said at the mosque, the place of worship for the community. Mosques are quite different from synagogues or churches; for example, they lack seats since part of the Salat prayer requires people to prostrate. Instead, thick carpet or prayer rugs are a common feature. Unlike in many churches or synagogues, men and women always pray separately in the mosque. Mosques also lack any artistic representations of God, people, or animals to protect against potential idolatry. Instead, mosques are often decorated with elaborate calligraphy or geometric art. Finally, the leader of the mosque, the imam, is not a specially trained member of the clergy but a respected community member who interprets the Qur'an and leads the prayers.

Sawm

The third of the Five Pillars is Sawm, the fast held during the month of Ramadan, the ninth month of the Islamic lunar calendar. According to tradition, during this month the Prophet received the first revelation of the Qur'an. The fast during Ramadan requires complete abstinence from food, drink, smoking, and sexual intercourse between sunrise and sunset for the entire twenty-eight day period. Instead, believers are to rest, pray, act charitably, and study the Qur'an starting at daybreak, which is determined by the ability to differentiate a white thread from a black thread. As soon as darkness has fallen, when the threads are indistinguishable, friends and family members gather to break the fast, often with great celebration. The month-long fast can be a rigorous ordeal, especially when Ramadan occurs in the long, hot daylight hours of the summer months. As such, pregnant or nursing women, children, and sick people are exempted from the fast for their own protection. At the end of the lunar month, Muslims hold a three day feast called the Eid al-Fitr, or the feast of fast-breaking.

Zakat

The fourth pillar is zakat, or acts of charity and kindness. Zakat involves giving a compulsory annual percentage of one's net worth to charity, though there is little agreement among Muslims over what that exact percentage may be. Zakat is interpreted broadly, with one of the few stipulations being that the money should go to help the poor and needy. They may donate to any charity or use their money however they choose, as long as the end result is to help those in need. Except for in a few Islamic states, no authority figure monitors zakat, and people are not expected to report their zakat giving to others; this obligation is strictly between the individual and Allah. Therefore, donations to the mosque to support daily operations are separate from zakat, which is distinctly charitable in nature.

Hajj

The fifth pillar is the Hajj, or pilgrimage to Mecca, which each Muslim should try to make once in his or her lifetime. The pilgrimage takes place during a five-day period of the final month of the Muslim lunar calendar. When pilgrims arrive, men trade their own clothes for a simple two-piece white garment. The simplicity of the garment reminds people that in the sacred precinct, no distinction is made between rich and poor. This is part of ihram, the state of purity required of all pilgrims. Women are not required to wear the white garment, but are encouraged to dress modestly. Believers circle the Ka'aba, a black stone housed in the Grand Mosque, and seek to touch or kiss it on their circumambulations. From there, believers move to the twin hills of Safa and Marwa, moving quickly back and forth between them to remember the story of Abraham's wife Hagar and her frantic search for water for her son Ishmael when they were exiled in the desert. In this story, Hagar's persistence is rewarded with a miraculous spring of water, the Zamzam spring, and pilgrims drink from this same spring. Next, people move to nearby Mount Arafat. For most of the day, the pilgrims fast, pray, and read the Qur'an at Arafat; this part of the pilgrimage anticipates the Day of Judgment, when at the end of time all people will stand and be judged by God, and is considered the most important day of the Hajj. Then pilgrims collect stones and cast them at several walls in Mina over the next few days; the walls represent the devil, and the ritual remembers Abraham's defeat of the devil when he made pilgrimage to that place. At this point, pilgrims will often return to the Ka'aba to once again circumambulate, and many will conclude with the sacrifice of an animal that is then eaten and shared with those in need. Those people who do not wish to perform the sacrifice themselves can commission another person to perform it on their behalf. When the pilgrim returns from the Hajj, she or he is called a hajji, an honorific title among Muslims.

Sometimes jihad is called the sixth pillar. Many misconceptions exist about jihad, beginning with the translation of the term. Though some people believe that jihad means "holy war," the true definition is "striving" or "struggle." Striving might take the form of defensive actions against enemies or persecutors, but jihad is just as likely to refer to a person's inner struggle against greed, selfishness, and error. In the hadith, traditional sayings of the Prophet, Muhammad is reported to have said, "The best jihad is the word of justice in front of the oppressive ruler."

Sacred Texts

The central, authoritative, and universally accepted sacred text of Islam is the Qur'an, which is also spelled Quran or Koran. The word Qur'an means "recitation," which invokes both the command of Jibril to Muhammad and the importance of reciting the Qur'an aloud. The Qur'an captures the revelations given to Muhammad during his meditations in the caves outside of Mecca (see "History"). The Prophet passed them on to the first Muslims, who wrote them down shortly after his death. For Muslims, a sign of the Qur'an's divine authority and inspiration is that Muhammad, though illiterate, could be the conduit for a text of such beauty and poetry. The Qur'an is also recognized as the final and complete revelation of the oneness of God, surpassing all previous revelations, including the Hebrew Bible and Christian New Testament. While Muslims do respect these texts as previous revelations from God, in places where the scriptures disagree, the Qur'an is always the final authority.

When the Qur'an was completed, there were 114 surahs, or chapters. With the exception of the first surah, the chapters are arranged roughly by length from longest to shortest and not chronologically by story, date, or revelation. Thus, when reading the Qur'an, one may notice that the story of the virgin birth of Jesus (Surah 19) appears before that of Noah (Surah 71). The words of the Qur'an are most authoritative in Arabic and in spoken form, and although translations are permissible, they are not considered to be perfectly inspired in the same way. Because of this emphasis, many Muslims strive to memorize and recite the Qur'an in Arabic. One who is able to commit the entire text to memory is known as a hafiz.

Sunni Muslims also recognize a collection of traditional sayings, actions, and silent approvals (sunnah) of the Prophet and his companions known as the hadith. There are thousands of individual hadith, which address a wide variety of legal and religious matters, and which also relate stories of the exemplary life of the Prophet. In Sunni Islam, these hadith are studied and discussed among scholars alongside the Qur'an, and their interpretations are used to help clarify proper day-to-day behavior. Shi'ite Muslims do not recognize the authority of the hadith.

Major Divisions

The two major divisions in Islam are rooted in an early dispute over succession following the death of the Prophet. At that time, he left no son to assume leadership, so the community elected leaders called caliphs to succeed him. The first three caliphs (abu-Bakr, Umar, and Uthman) were the Prophet's close friends; the fourth, named Ali, was his son-in-law. Ali was killed, as was his son and potential successor Husayn, by people associated with the caliphate. Muslims who wished to keep succession in the family of Muhammad saw Ali and Husayn as martyrs, which resulted in a permanent split. The group that followed the community-elected caliphs became known as Sunni, referring to the traditions, or sunnah, established by Muhammad; the followers of Ali who believed leadership should remain within Muhammad's family were called Shia, or Shi'ites. Sunni Muslims currently make up nearly ninety percent of the world's Islamic population. This is the dominant form of Islam in Saudi Arabia, North Africa, Afghanistan, Pakistan, Indonesia, and Central Asia. The largest Shi'ite population is in Iran, and majority populations are also in Azerbaijan, Bahrain, and Iraq.

Sunnis practice a form of Islam that recognizes the authority of the Qur'an and relies on the traditions (sunnah and hadith) of the Prophet to provide moral guidance (see "Sacred Texts"). Sunni communities

interpret these texts, a process known as *fiqh*, by means
of consensus, believing that God would not allow an
entire community to err in its interpretation. Sunni
communities also use the principle of analogy during *fiqh*,
responding to new situations by drawing parallels to older
interpretations. As a result, Sunni communities develop
different standards and laws (sharia) in different places
using these same principles. Four main schools of law
have developed from Sunni interpretive practice: Hanafi,
Maliki, Shafi'i and Hanbali. The interpretations by these
schools are divergent, ranging from traditional to liberal.
Therefore, sharia is not a singular, universal Islamic law.
Rather, sharia is a diverse set of laws with specifics that
are unique to the culture and community which have
interpreted them.

Shia Islam differs from Sunni in several important
ways. First, where Sunni Muslims seek consensus in the
development of community law, Shi'ites depend upon
the mandates of Imams. Imams (the capitalized word
is different from the lowercase "imam," which is simply
a mosque leader) were historical heads of the Shia sect,
beginning with Ali and continuing in his lineage for
twelve subsequent generations. These twelve Imams are
understood by Shi'ites to share the authority of Ali after
Muhammad's death; their directives to the community
are seen as absolute authority on all matters to this day.
One specific Shi'ite sect, called Twelvers, is uniquely
messianic in nature. Though the majority of Shi'ites are
Twelvers, not all Shi'ite Muslims are part of this sect.
Twelvers believe that the twelfth Imam, called al-Mahdi,
was taken to heaven in body prior to his death, and he

will someday return to participate in the judgment of the world. Though they still view Muhammad as the final prophet, Twelvers believe that the Mahdi will play an important role during the end times, so they wait expectantly for his return. In the meantime, the Mahdi guides the ayatollahs (high leaders within Twelver tradition) from his position in heaven.

Another key difference between the two sects is which sacred texts they accept. Whereas Sunni Muslims value the sunnah (as captured within the hadith) as an important source of morality and legislation, Shi'ites reject this tradition. From the Shi'ite perspective, the hadith are suspect because they do not mention Ali as the rightful successor to Muhammad, which is a fundamental tenet of Shi'ite belief. Since the sunnah plays such a key role in creating the diverse laws of Sunni communities, it is no surprise that Shi'ite communities lack similar legal diversity. Instead, relying on the ayatollahs, they employ a more hierarchical structure for the creation and enforcement of community regulations.

There is also a smaller sect known as Sufi, which can exist within either Sunni or Shi'ite traditions. Sufism is a mystical sect of Islam which emphasizes becoming one with God through prayer and meditation. The word "Sufi" is of uncertain origin, but may be related to the word *suf*, which means "wool" in Arabic and describes the simple garments of the Sufi. This movement grew out of a reaction to the growing political power of Islam in the eighth century as it began to spread. The main emphasis of Sufi mysticism is fana, or extinction of the self and total union with the divine. Fana is achieved through rigorous devotional and meditation practices, the best known of which is a whirling dance, which gives rise to the term "whirling dervishes" used to describe Sufi practitioners. The dervishes spin in place, arms extended, head to one side, seeking to overcome the separation between themselves and God in the ecstatic trance produced by this dance.

UNDERSTANDING ISLAM

Since September 11, 2001, there has been an increase in anti-Islamic sentiment in the United States. Even ten years later, the Pew Forum reports nearly forty percent of Americans have an unfavorable perception of Islam, and thirty-five percent believe Islam is more likely than other religions to encourage violence (http://pewforum. org/Muslim/Public-Remains-Conflicted-Over-Islam.aspx). Unfortunately, this bigotry simply displays ignorance; it recognizes neither the close connections between Muslims and other Western religions nor the diverse ways of being Muslim. Instead, the bias against Muslims is based on a stereotyped picture of Muslims as Arab terrorists who worship a foreign god. However, true Islam is a religion of finding peace through submission to the unified God of Jews, Christians, and Muslims through attention to one's inner and outer state. The largest group of Muslims in the world is not even from the Arabian Peninsula, but from Indonesia. While non-Muslims may not embrace Islam as their own faith, correcting these dangerous and ill-informed stereotypes is the first step in building avenues of trust among the three Abrahamic Religions.

FOR FURTHER READING

Arberry, A. J. *The Koran Interpreted: A Translation*. Austin: Touchstone, 1996.

Armstrong, Karen. *Muhmmad: A Prophet for Our Time*. New York: HarperOne, 2007.

Gottschalk, Peter and Gabriel Greenburg. *Islamophobia: Making Muslims the Enemy*. Lanham, MD: Rowman and Littlefield, 2008.

Nasr, Seyyed Hossein. *Islam: Religion, History and Civilization*. San Francisco: HarperSanFrancisco, 2003.

Pew Forum Research Center. "The Future of the Global Muslim Population." http://pewresearch.org/pubs/1872/muslim-population-projections-worldwide-fast-growth.

Sonn, Tamara. *A Brief History of Islam*. Oxford: Blackwell, 2004.

Hindu goddess

HINDUISM

INTRODUCTION

Hinduism is the world's third largest religion, and is also one of the oldest. The term *Hindu* itself refers to the Indus River. As travelers came into the area they began calling Indian people who were neither Muslim nor Christian "Hindu" because of their location. Over time, this collection of beliefs (now understood to be Hindu) crystallized within Indian society. Though India itself is a democratic country with official separation of church and state, the religious traditions of Hinduism are embedded in Indian society.

HISTORY

Hinduism's origin cannot be tied to one founder, but archaeologists have found evidence of a pre-Hindu civilization near the Indus River in part of modern Pakistan which dates back to around 3000 BCE. There are various theories about how Hinduism came to be, but it is likely a blending of the beliefs of Indo-European migrants into the region along with those of the preexisting Indian culture.

BELIEFS

At first glance, Hinduism may seem like a polytheistic tradition, but in reality we would classify it as monism. Monism is the belief that there is one essence or ultimate reality, Brahman, which is within many forms. This should not be confused with monotheistic traditions in which one god is worshiped. For monotheisms, the concept of god is intact and separate from all other spirits. For Hinduism, Brahman is so huge that it would be impossible to worship; therefore, Hindus worship many deities who represent different attributes of Brahman. By breaking down the parts of Brahman into many unique identities, Hindus are able to fully encounter the divine.

There are deities with humanlike appearances and those who look like animals, including Ganesha, the elephant-headed god who is the remover of obstacles. There are both male and female deities as well. Some deities are responsible for nature, like Indra, the god of storm. A hierarchy of gods exists and the top three are the Trimurti, often called the Hindu trinity. They represent the full circle of life: Brahma (not to be confused with Brahman) the creator, Vishnu the sustainer, and Shiva the destroyer.

Brahma sets the world into motion. He initiates the process, and then daily operations become the responsibility of Vishnu, who sustains existence with the help of Shiva. In Hinduism, there is no evil or hell, though there is an acknowledgement of demons. However, demons are not defined as evil; rather, they reject their religious duty (dharma) and instead act selfishly. This selfishness distinguishes them from the devas (the Hindu deities), who are flawed and sometimes make mistakes, but who still ultimately submit to dharma. So even though Shiva is the god of destruction, that does not mean that Shiva is evil; rather, this focus on destruction is merely an acknowledgment that things come to an end. Vishnu and Shiva work together in a partnership of preservation, destruction, and restoration. The many adventures of the Hindu deities are captured in a vast number of Hindu scriptures.

Sacred Scriptures

Hindus have two major bodies of scripture: sruti ("heard") and smriti ("remembered"). Hindus believe that the sruti was divinely revealed to holy men. The sruti includes the Vedas, which are the oldest Hindu texts, and the later addition of the Upanishads.

The smriti are scriptures attributed to human creation that are also respected and worshiped. These include the epic stories of the gods (Mahabharata and Ramayana), the Laws of Manu (civil code), and the Puranas (more mythology and genealogies of royal families).

The Vedas (literally meaning "truth") are written in Sanskrit and are divided into four sections: Rig (hymn) Veda, Yajur (ceremonial) Veda, Sama (chants) Veda, and Artharva (practical prayers) Veda. The Rig Veda is the oldest and considered to be the most important because it contains the stories of the creation of the universe.

Later there was a shift in the understanding of worship within the Upanishads, which means "sitting near." The Upanishads show intangible ways to worship the gods with hearts and minds rather than externally through chants, dances, or sacrifices.

The Upanishads also outline a basic understanding of the universe and set forth guidelines for how people should live their lives. Within the many forms of Brahaman, humans are included, and the human soul is called the atman. Each human being is born into samsara, which is the cycle of birth, life, death, and rebirth. While the atman is trapped within samsara, there is a universal law of action, karma, which drives behavior based on the individual's dharma, their duty or responsibility in life.

Karma is not just the idea of "what goes around comes around." For Hindus, the concept of karma is more complex. In a person's life, both positive and negative things happen as a natural consequence of that person's actions not only in this life, but in past lives as well. These positive and negative consequences are the result not necessarily of whether a person has been "good or bad," but rather of how well he or she has observed his or her religious duty, or dharma.

A person's dharma is determined based on his or her caste and life stage. Dharma will guide the choices of a person in gaining positive karma and minimizing negative karma. In the cycle of samsara, the atman is reincarnated and given repeated opportunities to build positive karma. Over several lifetimes, the atman that has eliminated negative karma will be liberated from samsara and reunited with Brahman. This liberation is called moksha.

One important idea in Hinduism is that of maya, or illusion. This world in which we are living is ultimately transitory. Therefore, one should not become too attached to the physical world and lose sight of the interconnectedness of existence. All is one. All is Brahman. This is the central reality of Hinduism. However, in their daily lives, many Hindus focus less on the quest for moksha and more on the life of the religion, which includes ritual practice, holiday celebrations, and community interaction.

Epics

The great epics make up one category of the many sacred Hindu texts, falling into the smriti tradition. Perhaps the most significant of these epics is called the Mahabharata, which is probably the longest epic poem in history. This epic focuses on the four most important life goals for a Hindu: dharma (duty), kama (pleasure), artha (success) and moksha (liberation). It tells the story of cousins, the Pandavas and Kauravas, who are fighting for the throne of the kingdom. The story is written so that the reader sympathizes with the Pandavas; the main character is Arjuna, the warrior prince who is leading his family to battle.

The sixteenth chapter of the Mahabharata is the Bhagavad Gita, one of the most famous and revered Hindu texts. Often called the Gita, this narrative centers on a dialogue between Arjuna and Krishna. Krishna is an avatar (another physical manifestation) of Vishnu, the preserver deity, but Arjuna does not realize that he is speaking with Krishna. Arjuna is conflicted about going to battle because he realizes that despite many years of war, nothing has been resolved. He knows that on the other side of the field his family will die in this battle. Krishna, disguised as his chariot driver, is both literally and figuratively taking Arjuna into battle. Krishna explains to Arjuna his responsibility to fulfill his dharma, which includes following his role as a warrior as well as seeking immortality of the soul.

Krishna also tells Arjuna that there are paths of yoga (union) with Brahman that he can practice to better understand his role in society and relationship to Brahman. The types of yoga are karma yoga (action union or good works), jñana yoga (wisdom union through the study of scriptures), raja yoga (meditation union), hatha yoga (energy union) and bhakti yoga (devotional union with the deities). Finally, Krishna reveals his identity to Arjuna. At that point, Arjuna falls to his knees in awe and makes his decision to fight.

The Ramayana, another great epic, follows another avatar of Vishnu named Rama. Rama is beloved in Hinduism because he is the ideal hero. Rama is born a warrior prince and is destined to inherit the throne of the kingdom of Ayodhya. His father, the king, is prepared to name him heir when one of his wives (not Rama's mother) comes and reminds him of a promise the king made her when he was very ill, and this wife was taking care of him. The king promised that her son Baharata would be heir. Upon hearing this, Rama encourages his father to honor his word. Rama agrees to leave Ayodhya along with his wife Sita and his other brother Lakshmana. They set up camp in the forest, and Rama leads a life of simplicity and humility, punctuated with occasional acts of heroism. For example, once he fights off a demon that has been attacking gurus (spiritual teachers) who live in the forest. This demon is actually a musician who is under a curse, and in defeating him, Rama lifts the curse and returns this demon to his human form.

At one point, Rama leaves Sita alone, and the evil demon king Ravana kidnaps her. When Rama returns, he sees that Sita is missing and begins to look for her. With the help of the loyal monkey king Sugriva and the monkey-deity Hanuman, Sita is rescued from the land of Lanka. After Hanuman safely returns Sita to Rama, Hanuman has his army build a bridge for Rama to cross so that Rama can go battle Ravana once and for all, ultimately defeating the demon king. Afterward, Rama questions Sita's purity after her long stay in another man's house, and as a result, Sita endures a "trial by fire," willingly entering a pyre to prove herself. She exits the fire unscathed, thus defending her purity to Rama, and they all return to Aydhoya. Their return marks the celebration of Diwali, the festival of lights, which commemorates the lamps that lined their path home.

Worship

The Upanishads outline a shift in the way Hindus worship from the external expression of faith to one that is more inwardly focused. There is not one specific day on which Hindus worship. Instead, they worship any day of the week in a mandir, or temple. Some temples create individual schedules of communal worship, but most are open all the time. Practitioners can stop by to worship on their own at any time. Priests will do ritual worship called puja to the deities on behalf of the community every day.

Puja takes many forms, from simple prayers or mediation to bathing and dressing of the deities. Most mandirs are dedicated to one specific deity. Many temples are dedicated to either Vishnu or Shiva because of their significance in everyday life. Priests keep the deities happy in the temples because the belief is that the shrines are the homes for the gods, and if they are not protected, the gods will abandon the temples. Most temples typically contain images dedicated to the central deity of the temple. For Hindus, the physical images of the gods are understood to be representations of the one larger essence of Brahman. In worshipping before these images, Hindus are showing their submission to this larger reality, not worshipping the image itself.

Most Hindu families also have household shrines. The household shrine typically is devoted to one central deity and contains a picture or statue of that deity. The family will put pictures of deceased loved ones, flowers, and incense around the shrine to honor the deity. The family will also perform puja to the deity, which entails saying prayers or chants, and sometimes leaving food for the deity. In both temple and home puja, people bathe and dress the deities as a sign of respect, praise, love, and thankfulness.

The popularity of certain household deities was traditionally based on geographic location. Each village would have a particular deity, but as villages grew, regions began to influence each other. Today the family, not the village, determines which deity will be at the center of the household shrine. Other deities, depending on need, can also be included on the shrine. For example, Ganesha, the remover of obstacles, is a popular deity to call upon in times of adversity.

The concept of yoga is also part of worshipping in Hinduism. Yoga, related to the concept of union, refers to various pathways of union with Brahman. In the United States, yoga usually refers to an exercise done in a gym. This type of yoga is called hatha yoga, or "force" yoga. Hatha yoga is the practice of balancing the physical body's components and aligning the breath of self with the ultimate breath of life. Yoga is only one among many possible pathways to union with Brahman.

There are four other yogic paths to union with Brahman: karma yoga, jñana yoga, raja yoga, and bhakti yoga. Karma yoga is the practice of charity or action union, emphasizing good works. Jñana yoga is practicing the knowledge that underlies the truth of reality, the difference between our ever-changing physical existence and the eternal nature of Brahman. This yoga is often understood to be more of an academic quest. Raja yoga is striving for union with Brahman through meditation and mental focus. Finally, bhakti yoga is the path to union by devotion to the deities at the temple and through home puja. A person could practice any or all of these forms of yoga.

Sects

Two important sects in Hinduism are Vaishnavism, focusing on Vishnu, or Shaivism, focusing on Shiva. Another sect called Shaktism focuses on the divine feminine aspect, the many powerful forms of Shakti.

In Vaishnavism, people worship the ten incarnations of Vishnu. Each time Vinshu comes to the earth, his mission is to help humanity. This concept of incarnation shapes the relationship between humans and Vishnu. Vaishnavites believe that Vishnu is a personal god and strive to develop a relationship with him. Typically, a Vaishnavite can be distinguished by the white marking on their forehead in the shape of a "V" with a red dot in the center representing Vishnu's wife Lakshmi.

Practitioners of Shaivism believe in Shiva as the supreme god. Though widely known as the god of destruction, Shiva is also simultaneously recreating. For example, sometimes forests are set on fire in order to stimulate new growth; similarly, Shiva's destructive actions create opportunities for new life to arise. Shaivites understand Shiva to be separate and different from humans. Traditionally, Shaivites are seen with three horizontal lines, symbolic of the Trimurti, on their foreheads. A red vertical line in the center symbolizes Shiva's all-knowing nature.

Shaktism focuses on Shakti (the divine feminine energy) in the form of the goddess, who has many names. Shakti is the Mother Goddess, the creative force of the universe, the essence of fertility, and the complement to the masculine energy of Shaivism or Vaishnavism. Shakti has many forms, including Parvati (the kind mother-goddess), Durga (the warrior goddess), and Kali (the goddess of destruction).

Even though each of these sects focuses upon a particular deity, most Hindus also worship other deities and participate in puja to these deities as well. For example, the celebration of Durga Puja is a popular festival which honors the change of season at the beginning of autumn, with Durga as the central deity. The festival is most commonly celebrated in South India.

Holidays and Festivals

Not all holidays are celebrated by all Hindus. Sometimes celebrations are geographically based, and sometimes the celebrations are practiced by a particular sect of Hinduism. For example, Shaivites would celebrate Shiva Ratri, which is an all night worship of Shiva, whereas Vaishnavites would celebrate Rama Navami (the worship of Rama) or Krishna Janmashtami, which is the celebration of the birthday of Krishna.

Many holidays are based on the stories of the deities. For example, Diwali is one of the most widely celebrated holidays and is based on the Ramayana. Diwali, the festival of lights, is considered a homecoming for Rama and Sita, and the affirmation of life's renewal. Some say that the celebration of light is also the recognition of the atman within, or one's divine light. This is a time when families exchange gifts and gather together for celebrations.

Other holidays focus on certain aspects of nature. For example, Holi is the spring festival, sometimes called the festival of colors. Traditionally, this festival has a youthful and joyous spirit, sometimes including friendly pranks and the tossing of colored powder on one another. This innocent play is in honor of the god Krishna and his wife Radha, who represent romantic, childlike love.

DEMOGRAPHICS

There are more than 800 million Hindus worldwide. More than eighty percent of Indians are Hindu compared to less than one percent of Americans.

*Student monks in
Kathmandu, Nepal*

Buddhism

INTRODUCTION

In the late sixth century CE, the majority of India's people were what today we would call Hindu, as there was no other recognized religion at the time. The highest caste in Hinduism was the priestly caste, the brahmins. Traditionally, priests were the communicators with the gods and the most educated people in society. As a result, brahmins held a great deal of power. In northern India, the impoverished lower castes were frustrated by their quality of life because of the rigidity of the caste system. Additionally, people often resorted to extreme practices of self-denial in order to achieve spiritual liberation. This was the world that Siddhartha, the founder of Buddhism, was born into, and within this unrest, Buddhism flourished.

Buddhism rejects the caste system and strives for equality among its believers. Whether young or old, male or female, black or white, each individual is capable of achieving enlightenment, or nirvana.

HISTORY

Siddhartha Gautama was born in 563 BCE in northern India, close to Nepal. His parents were King Sudhodana and Queen Mahamaya, who were members of the kshatriya caste of warriors and rulers.

According to tradition, there were several miraculous occurrences surrounding Siddhartha's conception and birth. For example, Queen Mahamaya dreamed that a white elephant with shiny, white, ivory tusks descended from the heavens and pierced her abdomen full of light. When she woke up the next morning, she mentioned her odd dream to the king. The king took her to the guru (spiritual teacher) to interpret the dream. The guru looked at her and told her she was with child. Queen Mahamaya's dream is known as the White Elephant Dream, or the immaculate conception of Siddhartha. Additionally, many Buddhists believe that Queen Mahamaya's pregnancy was miraculously ideal and that the birth was painless, and also that Siddhartha came into the world able to walk and talk.

During the child's traditional naming ceremony, a holy man named Asita looked into the eyes of Siddhartha and predicted that Siddhartha could someday be "the master of the universe," a great king above all kings. However, Asita also warned King Sudhodana that if Siddhartha ever encountered suffering, he would be overcome with compassion and would become a great spiritual leader instead of a great king. As a result of the prophecy, the king tried to prevent Siddhartha from encountering suffering by providing everything he needed or wanted within the walls of the palace.

As Siddhartha grew, he became a householder and started a family. Though he was materially successful, he still felt that something was missing. Therefore, with the help of a chariot driver, Siddhartha left the palace for the first time. In the town, Siddhartha encountered four sights which changed his life. For the first time, Siddhartha witnessed aging, illness, and death. As he wrestled with his new awareness of suffering, he saw a fourth sight—a holy man. This man seemed content, even though he had nothing. Siddhartha asked the man how he possibly could be content while so much suffering existed in the world. The holy man explained that he had taken a vow of renunciation and had dedicated his life to seeking enlightenment. These experiences moved Siddhartha, so he left the palace, his wife, and his child forever.

For the next six years, Siddhartha became a renunciant, which meant living with no possessions and engaging in extreme ascetic practices. By trying to minimize his focus on physical comfort and the material world, he hoped to transcend his present existence and achieve enlightenment. Siddhartha practiced fasting and holding his breath for extended periods of time. These extreme practices brought him close to death, but failed to bring him closer to enlightenment. This led Siddhartha to realize one of the most important concepts in Buddhism: the doctrine of the Middle Way. After living his life at both ends of the spectrum from extreme pleasure to extreme asceticism, he realized extremes are not the answer. He began to believe that enlightenment is only possible when both the body and the soul are well.

One day he sat underneath a sacred fig tree, also known as the Bodhi Tree, the tree of enlightenment. He was determined not to move from that point until he had achieved nirvana. Buddhist tradition tells us that Siddhartha began to transcend his current physical reality and entered a spiritual realm where he encountered a series of temptations by Mara, the Lord of Death. After successfully defeating Mara, Siddhartha finally confronted an image of his own powerful ego, and he responded, "Let the Earth be my witness. You are an illusion." This declaration allowed him to achieve nirvana. In his state of enlightenment, he saw all his past lives and understood the nature of the cycle of life, death, and rebirth (samsara). Siddhartha was awakened, and from that point he became the Buddha, "the enlightened one."

The Buddha felt compelled to share what he had learned. He delivered a sermon to a group of ascetic skeptics, who were still living the extreme life that the Buddha had rejected. Others called this sermon "Setting in Motion the Wheel of Dharma" because the Buddha explained the problem of suffering as well as the solution. He explained how people can bring an end to suffering and how all people were capable of achieving enlightenment. These ascetics became his disciples, and they began to share his teachings as well.

BELIEFS

Buddhism is a very systematic religion; one major concept leads to another. Even though the Buddha paved a path that led to his own enlightenment, this path may be different for each person. One of the essential teachings of the Buddha was that everyone's path is unique.

The Three Marks of Existence

The Three Marks of Existence are universal truths that apply to all being. These are:

1. Anatta, or "no ego," means that there is no personal or eternal soul. It is consciousness that is reincarnated, not the soul.

2. Anicca, or impermanence, means that all things are constantly changing, and change cannot be stopped. In the same way that the essence of a river cannot be captured, neither can anything be captured in existence.

3. Dukkha, often translated as "suffering," results from the impermanence of the material world. Nothing we grow attached to will last forever, and we will only suffer when it is gone.

The Four Noble Truths

Just as a diagnosis points to a disease and a prescription offers the solution, the Four Noble Truths explain the problem of suffering and then describe the solution.

1. The First Noble Truth: To live life is to suffer. No one can escape suffering because there is no ego and everything is constantly changing.

2. The Second Noble Truth: The cause of suffering is desire (tanha) and attachment to the physical world. All different types of desire, whether for people, possessions, or things you wish to own, cause suffering.

3. The Third Noble Truth: To end suffering, it is necessary to end desire and attachment.

4. The Fourth Noble Truth: One must follow the Eightfold Path, a set of ideal practices to minimize desire, thereby minimizing one's suffering.

Some people question the desire to achieve enlightenment and how that fits in with larger Buddhist ideals. The idea is that each person should be smart about the types of desires in his or her life. Desires for popularity or financial success ideally will be replaced by the desire to seek enlightenment. Since desire is innately human, there is no way to completely eliminate it, but one can reduce the negative impact of desire in one's life, ultimately reducing human suffering.

The Eightfold Path

The Eightfold Path looks like a code of conduct, and traditionally the list has been translated with each path beginning with the word "right." However, a better translation may be, "Try the very best that you can." The Eightfold Path is usually represented by an eight-spoked wheel, a traditional symbol of Buddhism. This wheel is often called the Wheel of Dharma, referring to the enduring nature of Buddhist truths. Additionally, the circular shape of the wheel invokes an awareness of samsara, the cycle of rebirth from which the Eightfold Path promises release. The eight spokes of the wheel correspond with the categories of wisdom (1, 2), ethical conduct (3, 4, 5), and concentration (6, 7, 8).

1. Right Understanding: By accepting the Three Marks of Existence and the Four Noble Truths, one is able to see things as they really are.

2. Right Intention: This intention is threefold, with intents to renounce desire, to act with good will, and to do no harm. These are required in order to put one's "right understanding" into action.

3. Right Speech: One should avoid lying, slander, and gossip.

4. Right Action: One should also avoid cheating, stealing, killing, and sexual misconduct.

5. Right Livelihood: One should earn a living honestly, peacefully, and legally, choosing an occupation that supports the Eightfold Path and does not hinder it. For example, hunting involves killing animals for food, so being a hunter directly contradicts Right Action.

6. Right Effort: This is a fourfold endeavor to avoid developing new negative qualities, to overcome existing negative qualities, to develop new positive qualities, and to maintain those positive qualities which already exist within oneself.

7. Right Mindfulness: Directing one's consciousness to stay fully focused on the present with detachment and complete attention.

8. Right Concentration: Expanding awareness through the frequent practice of meditation.

Buddhism is a universal religion because many Buddhists believe that their beliefs can be applicable to all people, and that anyone who dedicates his or her life to following the Eightfold Path and lives a life of moderation can reach nirvana. Consequently, there are some Buddhists who reach out to others in order to help them also become Buddhist.

DEMOGRAPHICS

Buddhism is the fourth largest religion in the world. Though most Buddhists live in Asia, Buddhism is a worldwide religion. There are three major schools of Buddhism: Theravada, Mahayana, and Vajrayana.

Theravada: "The Way of the Elders"

Theravada Buddhists are the most orthodox; they consider themselves to be the branch which follows most closely to the Buddha's teachings. They are strict followers of the scripture called the Tripitaka, which translates as "three baskets." The Tripitaka is separated into three sections. First is the Vinaya Pitaka, containing laws governing monks and nuns. The second section is the Sutta Pitaka, which holds the teachings of the Buddha. Within the Sutta Pitaka is the Dhammapada—literally, "path,"—the most well-known Buddhist scripture containing teachings about how Buddhists should live their lives and broad truths about the universe. The final portion is the Abhidamma, which contains metaphysical commentaries on the Buddha's teaching. The Tripitaka is written in the Pali language and is often called the Pali Canon. This collection is revered by the Theravada community but not necessarily by other Buddhists.

The majority of Theravada Buddhists are monks and nuns who have dedicated their lives to achieving nirvana. Theravada Buddhists believe that the Buddha was an average man with extraordinary accomplishments. They dedicate their lives to following in the Buddha's footsteps. Because of the strict commitment that is required,

Theravada Buddhists believe that only a few people will be able to achieve nirvana in this lifetime. However, those who remain will be reincarnated and have the opportunity to continue along the path to enlightenment. Sometimes Mahayana Buddhists refer to Theravada Buddhism as Hinayana, or the lesser vehicle. Theravada Buddhists consider this term to be derogatory.

Mahayana: "The Great Vehicle"

Mahayana Buddhist are the most widespread and diverse group. There are many different types of Mahayana Buddhists, including Zen and Pure Land. One significant difference between Mahayana and Theravada is the veneration of Bodhisattvas. Some Mahayana Buddhists believe that bodhisattvas are "enlightened beings" who achieved nirvana in their lifetime, but who chose to be reincarnated in order to help other people achieve nirvana. Other Mahayana Buddhists consider bodhisattvas to be those who have taken the vow to achieve enlightenment and have pledged to help all sentient beings along the way. There are also many different buddhas—those who have reached nirvana—in Mahayana Buddhism. Additionally, whereas Theravada Buddhists consider the Buddha to be an ordinary man with extraordinary qualities, Mahayana Buddhists believe in the Buddha's divine nature, making him different from the average person. Therefore, the path to nirvana is more difficult for ordinary people because the Buddha's nature makes him impossible to fully emulate.

Vajrayana: "The Diamond Vehicle"
or "The Thunderbolt Vehicle"

Vajrayana Buddhism, also known as Tibetan Buddhism or esoteric Buddhism, has gained high visibility worldwide thanks to their leader Tenzin Gyatso, also known as the 14th Dalai Lama. Tibetan Buddhists believe that the Dalai Lama is a reincarnation of the bodhisattva Avalokiteshvara, "the compassionate one." They believe that Avalokiteshvara has been reincarnated lifetime after lifetime as the Dalai Lama in order to lead and serve the Tibetan Buddhist people throughout history. Vajrayana traditions are unique in that they incorporate mystical traditions and magical practices. Tibetan Buddhists engage the senses through mandalas (circular art), mudras (hand positions), and mantras (chants), allowing a person to recognize his or her humanity in a paradoxical attempt to let go of humanity during meditation.

*The Golden Temple
of Amritsar, India*

SIKHISM

INTRODUCTION

In the tradition of Sikhism, the word Sikh means "disciple." The sacred symbol of Sikhism, the khanda, captures their history and central beliefs. The khanda has a double-edged sword in the center, representing the duality of the individual as both soldier and saint. Swords, called kirpans, cross on the outside, representing spiritual and physical strength. At the center is a chakkar, or circle, symbolizing the unity of all people and the belief in one god.

HISTORY

The Sikh religion has a single religious founder named Guru Nanak, but a series of gurus, or spiritual teachers, firmly established the faith after Nanak's death. Guru Nanak was born in 1469 CE in Punjab, a province in northern India. He was born into a higher caste of Hinduism (see Hinduism). A narrative story called the Janamsakhi explains that Nanak's birth was special. According to tradition, he was born in a mud hut in the middle of the night. At the moment of his birth, the hut filled with light. There was a prediction that he would be a prophet that united many faiths. Stories of his childhood say he spread peace and love to all he encountered, and then as a young man, he received a calling. One day he went to the nearby river to bathe, but then he mysteriously disappeared. His family went to look for him but found only his clothes. They believed Nanak had drowned. Three days later, Nanak reappeared and revealed that the one divine essence of the universe spoke to him. God blessed him and sent him out into the world as a prophet. Nanak's response was, "There is no Hindu. There is no Muslim" (see Islam). Nanak emphasized the concept of monotheism and rejection of the caste system. He wrote poetry and hymns praising God. At the end of his life, he called upon one of his disciples and renamed him Angad, which means "a part of my own self." Nanak believed that this renaming was a spiritual awakening for Angad which would allow him to succeed Nanak as the second guru.

Angad wrote poetry and began signing it with the pseudonym Nanak. He also developed a written language for the regional dialect of the Punjabi language called Gurmukhi. Before his death, Angad named Amar Das as the third guru. Amar Das continued to write, and he envisioned a place of worship to be built in Amritsar. Then the fourth guru, Ram Das, actually began building the Golden Temple at Amritsar, as Amar Das had envisioned.

The fifth guru, Arjan, wrote more than 1,000 hymns. He was responsible for collecting the writings of the gurus into the sacred book, the *Adi Granth*. He divided the book into various sections by raga, or "melody." For example, the first raga is Sri ("supreme"); thus, all the writings in that section praise the supremacy of the one God. The *Adi Granth* was completed on August 16, 1604. The Golden Temple was completed shortly thereafter. At that time, people in the surrounding society considered Sikhs to be a threat. As a result, Arjan was imprisoned and tortured to death, making him the first martyr of the faith. This event shifted the nature of Sikhism from nonviolence to aggression as the Sikhs fought back against persecution with violence. Arjan's son and the sixth guru, Har Gobind, led this transition.

Har Gobind began to dress like a warrior and carried two swords after his father's death. The sword of spiritual power was called the piri, and the sword of physical power was the miri. Har Gobind decided that Sikhs should abandon the principle of ahimsa (nonviolence) to protect themselves from violent persecution. The ninth guru, Tegh Bahadur, was imprisoned and decapitated by a Muslim emperor who believed the Sikhs were a threat to Islamic culture and power. The tenth guru, Gobind Rai, responded by emphasizing physical power.

Gobind Rai created a military group of Sikhs called Khalsa ("pure ones"). Part of Gobind Rai's inner circle formed the first Khalsa, and these people distinguished themselves by using five outward symbols beginning with K, often called the "Five Ks":

1. Kes: All kes, or hair, remains uncut because hair is considered to be a sacred gift.

2. Kirpan: One must carry a sword called a kirpan, which represents a willingness to fight for religious liberty and to protect the helpless.

3. Kangha: A kangha, or comb, is worn underneath the turban to symbolize the importance of cleanliness.

4. Kachera: The kachera is a type of undergarment worn by warriors, and it reminds the wearer to maintain self-control.

5. Kara: The kara, a special bracelet, shows the infinite union of God and strength through its symbolic circular shape.

Both men and women in the Khalsa wore the Five Ks, and continue to wear them today. Gobind Rai's focus on military service earned him the name Gobind Singh (literally "Gobind the Lion"). His four sons were killed in battle, leaving no suitable successor. He feared imprisonment, which would have left the Sikhs without a leader. As a result, Gobind Rai declared that the final and everlasting guru would be the *Adi Granth* instead of a person, which is why the *Adi Granth* is now often called the Guru Granth Sahib.

BELIEFS

Though some people argue that Sikhism is a blending of Islamic and Hindu beliefs, this is not completely correct. While Sikhs are monotheistic like Muslims, and though they believe in reincarnation like Hindus, Sikh beliefs and traditions are unique and contain many aspects that are unlike either Hinduism or Islam.

The place of worship in Sikhism is the gurdwara. Every sanctuary has a special altar for the *Adi Granth*. Sikhism has no hierarchal leadership; therefore, anyone can read from the sacred text or lead worship. At the heart of the gurdwara is the langar, which refers to the kitchen where the sacred community meal is served—not just to

Sikhs, but to all who need to eat, regardless of religion, gender, or social class. Believers take turns doing seva (selfless service, or a deed of love for the congregation) by serving in the langar, preparing and serving food for the community. Langar is an essential part of Sikh communal life, as it demonstrates the centrality of inclusivity and social outreach.

Sikhs openly reject the caste system and embrace equality. The sangat, or community, is at the center of the faith. Guru Nanak once said, "One disciple is a single Sikh, two a holy association, but five, there is ultimate reality itself!" Traditionally, Sikhs disregard gender and social status when they sit in long rows on the sanctuary floor (pangats).

The *Adi Granth* does not include any historical narratives or codes of behavior, nor does it outline any requirements. Instead, the *Adi Granth* primarily reinforces the belief in one amazing and supreme god. The first few words are also at the core of the Sikh creed: "There is one Being." The goal of life for a Sikh is to remove the individual ego and cease the cycle of reincarnation to reunite with the One.

DEMOGRAPHICS

Sikhism is the fifth largest world religion with close to 30 million believers. The largest population of Sikhs is in the north Indian state of Punjab, though a significant number of Sikhs also live in Great Britain. There were two main motivations for migration in the nineteenth century. One was the Sikh requirement for military service, and the other was the attack in 1984 when the Indian army desecrated the Golden Temple.

FOR FURTHER READING

www.sikhs.org

BAHA'I

INTRODUCTION

The Baha'i faith is one of the newest global religious traditions. The Baha'i faith developed out of Islamic culture in Iran, so many Muslims consider the Baha'is to be a heretical group. There are reports of Baha'is being persecuted for their beliefs to this day. In spite of this tension, there are clearly some Islamic influences in Baha'i beliefs and practices like monotheism, the rejection of alcohol, and a month of fasting and purification. However, distinctions between the two traditions are significant, including the lack of ritualism, acceptance of progressive revelation, and a diversity of sacred texts among the Baha'is.

HISTORY

The beginnings of the Baha'i faith can be traced to an Iranian man named Siyyid Ali Muhammad, who was known as the Bab, meaning "the gate." The Bab preached the coming of a new messenger of God who would bring a message of unity and peace for all people. Muslims considered his messianic preachings to be not only treason but blasphemy because of the central Islamic belief that Muhammad is the final prophet from God—the "Seal of the Prophets." The Bab was imprisoned and executed in 1850.

Shortly after the Bab's execution, a Babi follower named Mirza Husayn Ali continued the Bab's proclamation and was jailed in Tehran, where he began to receive direct revelations from God. Through these revelations, Ali learned that he was the messenger the Bab had been predicting and therefore became known as Baha'u'llah ("Glory of God"). Due to his controversial claims, he was eventually ejected from Iran, and while in exile he wrote letters and scriptures emphasizing one central idea: the complete harmony of humankind. After Baha'u'llah died, his son and then grandson continued to preach the faith.

BELIEFS

Baha'is believe in a long line of prophets including (but not restricted to) Abraham, Moses, David, Zoroaster, Krishna, the Buddha, Jesus, Muhammad, and finally Baha'u'llah. Because all of these prophets are unique reflections of the same singular God, Baha'is understand that all religions come from the same spiritual source. Different revelations from different prophets are dependent upon the special cultural needs of people throughout history. The religion teaches that, unfortunately, it is culture itself that has distorted the revelations of God, resulting in conflict among religious traditions. God in the Baha'i faith is the source of all creation, and though described as a "personal God" in Baha'i scriptures, God is also an unknowable entity who is accessible only through the prophets sent to help humanity. Baha'is believe that God will continue to send prophets until the end of time.

Typically, Baha'is meet in each other's homes for worship and fellowship, though there are also many Baha'i community centers located across the globe. There are very few official Baha'i temples worldwide; each continent houses only one significant Baha'i temple. In the United States, the Baha'i temple is located in Wilmette, Illinois. Each temple has nine sides to coincide with the nine-pointed star which is the symbol of the faith.

The Baha'i calendar was created by the Bab, who broke the year into nineteen months consisting of nineteen days each. On the first day of each month, the Baha'i community gathers together. The last month in the religious calendar (March 2–20) is one of fasting and renewal. During these ten days, Baha'is fast from sunrise to sunset; then at the conclusion of the fast, March 21 marks the New Year, which is a time for renewal. Other significant holidays are those commemorating the births of the Bab and Baha'u'llah. Baha'is have no sacraments and few specific rituals, with the exceptions of marriage, funeral, and daily prayer rites.

Most Bah'ais practice the observance of nine holy days, participation in the month of fasting, and dedication to fighting inequality. Additionally, many Baha'is enjoy making pilgrimage to the shrine of the Bab in Israel and refrain from consumption of alcohol. The sacred texts of the Baha'i faith are mostly attributed to Baha'u'llah. Some are in the form of letters, while others are meditations or prayers. The most prominent scripture is the Kitáb-i-Aqdas, The Most Holy Book. In addition to the Baha'i literature, sacred texts of other religious traditions are also accepted. In Baha'i tradition, the concepts of heaven and hell refer to the distance between the soul and God, not to places of reward and punishment. The farther away from God someone is, the more that person is in hell. For Baha'is, the human soul is immortal, and they aim to improve the soul by improving life for all people by promoting equality, ending poverty, and advocating universal education. Baha'u'llah said, "The Earth is but one country and humankind its citizens," reflecting his dedication to global peace.

DEMOGRAPHICS

There are over 7 million practicing Baha'is worldwide. There is no ordained leadership in the Baha'i faith; decisions are made by group consensus. There are small local assemblies who make community decisions, as well as an international governing body called the Universal House of Justice, located in Israel. National Spiritual Assemblies supervise the affairs of each country.

FOR FURTHER READING

http://www.bahai.us/bahai-temple

WORLD TRADITIONS COMPARED

	NATURE OF GOD	NATURE OF HUMANITY	NATURE OF THE UNIVERSE	NATURE OF RELIGION	FOUNDERS AND TEXTS
CHRISTIANITY	One creator-God in three persons: Father, Son, and Holy Spirit. God is personal, interacts with humanity, is all-knowing, and all-powerful.	God allows humans free will to choose between right and wrong. However, they are inherently sinful and are incapable of achieving salvation on their own. Ultimately, salvation only comes through God.	This world is temporary. We are engaged in a battle between good and evil. Someday God will judge all people at the end of time, which will bring the long-awaited coming of the "Kingdom of God."	Through belief in Jesus Christ, humans are saved from sin and will have eternal life after death. Because Jesus is the supreme sacrifice to atone for the sins of humanity, Christianity is the only path to salvation.	The founders were followers of Jesus of Nazareth, born sometime between 7 BCE and 1 CE. Texts include the Bible (including Old and New Testaments) and, for some Christians, the Apocrypha.
JUDAISM	One singular creator-God (YHWH, or Yahweh) who is simultaneously personal and unknowable.	Humans have free will to choose between good and evil; human beings are not born into sin. Humans are created in God's image, and all who do good have a place in God's kingdom—though the Jewish people are uniquely chosen as God's people.	Judaism lacks a strong focus on an afterlife, so people concentrate more on life in the present world. Jews look to a coming messiah who will restore Israel and usher in an era of peace. They also anticipate a future day of resurrection.	Judaism is defined more by action and cultural identity than specific belief; there are a variety of individual interpretations. The heart of religion is ethical action, supported by the traditions of Moses, the prophets, and previous Jewish generations throughout history.	According to Jewish tradition Judaism began with the covenant between God and Abraham, when God declares Abraham's descendants to be the chosen people. Two well-known texts are the Tanakh (called the Old Testament in Christianity) and the Talmud, containing laws and commentaries. There are also many additional texts.

WORLD TRADITIONS COMPARED *continued*

	NATURE OF GOD	NATURE OF HUMANITY	NATURE OF THE UNIVERSE	NATURE OF RELIGION	FOUNDERS AND TEXTS
ISLAM	One singular creator-god (Allah) who is personal and interacts directly with humanity. Muslims equate Allah with the god of Judaism and Christianity.	Humans were created to praise Allah, and that should be each person's greatest goal. Each person has free will to choose whom to serve, and therefore is accountable for his or her own actions. All who submit to Allah will see paradise in the afterlife.	This world is a testing ground for human beings, where their true nature will be proven by their choices. Muslims look to a final day when Allah will judge all people, when the dead will be resurrected, and when the world as we know it will end.	The Qur'an is the greatest and final revelation in a succession of previous revelations. By adhering to the Five Pillars and following Qur'anic law (Sharia), humans may gain peace through submission to Allah.	Muhammad, who received his first revelation in 610 CE, is believed to be a descendant of Abraham through Ishmael. The most sacred text is the Qur'an, and some Muslims also accept hadith (words, actions, and approvals of Muhammad).
HINDUISM	One all-encompassing being (Brahman) with many faces and manifestations (avatars). The deities are imperfect, but they still ultimately model submission to religious duty (dharma).	Humans are trapped in the cycle of rebirth (samsara), which they may escape over many lifetimes. One ascends this ladder through submission to dharma, which includes submission to the deities.	The universe is engaged in a never-ending cycle of creation, destruction, and renewal. The present world is in a state of decline; eventually, it will be destroyed and a new universe will be reborn in its place.	If people follow dharma, the deities will assist in their paths to liberation (moksha). Dharma fights chaotic forces, so religion maintains universal order and discourages people from acting selfishly.	There is no founding prophet; ancient Indo-European religion merged with indigenous religion to form diverse Hindu traditions. There are many sacred texts, including the Vedas, Puranas, Upanishads, and epics.

	NATURE OF GOD	NATURE OF HUMANITY	NATURE OF THE UNIVERSE	NATURE OF RELIGION	FOUNDERS AND TEXTS
BUDDHISM	Generally nontheistic, meaning there is no concept of God. Some Buddhist sects include veneration of the Buddha and/or bodhisattvas. Others include belief in deities who—like humans—are also on the road to enlightenment.	Humans have no-self and no-soul. Life is filled with suffering, springing from attachment to the material world. By freeing oneself from attachment through the Eightfold Path, one may escape suffering and reach enlightenment.	The entire material world is an illusion. Boundaries that separate humans from each other—and from all sentient beings—are also illusory. All beings are connected, which should prompt people to treat all with compassion.	The Buddha demonstrated how to travel the road to enlightenment via the "Middle Path," which all may follow. Upon enlightenment, humans break free from rebirth and reach nirvana, dissolving into oneness with the universe like a drop of water uniting with the ocean.	Siddhartha Gautama, The Buddha, was born in 623 BCE and was the first to achieve enlightenment. The Sutras are the most sacred Buddhist texts, though there are also many other texts. Some Buddhists reject texts altogether to avoid attachment to the material world.
SIKHISM	One supreme creator-god who is personal and interacts with humanity, but who is also simultaneously transcendent and beyond human understanding.	Humans are easily distracted by the physical world, so they remain trapped in the cycle of reincarnation. However, dedication to god and a spiritual focus will lead to salvation in the afterlife.	Attachment to the material world distracts from spirituality and separates humans from God. True reality is intangible, and can only be perceived with the heart. Good works in the material world should spring from this awareness.	Religious practice (especially meditation) allows humans to connect with God. Religion should unite people, not divide them. Focus is not just on salvation in the afterlife, but also charity, community, and family in this life.	Guru Nanak founded Sikhism during the 15th century CE. A succession of other gurus (teacher-leaders) succeeded him, with the tenth and final guru being the Adi Granth, the holy scripture of Sikhism.

WORLD TRADITIONS COMPARED *continued*

NATURE OF GOD	NATURE OF HUMANITY	NATURE OF THE UNIVERSE	NATURE OF RELIGION	FOUNDERS AND TEXTS
One creator-god who has sent unique revelations to different peoples in culturally specific ways. Though god is inaccessible, god is knowable through the prophets.	Humanity is radically one; divisions among people are artificial and destructive. The purpose of humanity is to love and serve god. Those who do will continue to be near god spiritually in the afterlife.	The world cycles through different ages, with each new prophet ushering in a new age of prosperity. Then over time the world declines, and a new prophet is necessary. Baha'is look to a future Golden Age marked by peace and unity of all humanity.	All religions are one. Differences among religions are created by humans, whereas similarities reveal divine truths. In progressive revelation throughout history, different prophets have shared unique aspects of God's truth with humanity.	Baha'u'llah (originally Mirza Husayn-Ali Nuri) founded the Baha'i Faith in 19th century CE. His many writings are all considered divine revelation. Among the most well-known are the *Kitab-i-Aqdas*, *Kitab-i-Iquan*, *Gleanings*, and the *Hidden Words*.

BAHA'I FAITH

RELIGIONS OF PLACE

TAOISM

INTRODUCTION

Taoism, or Daoism (pronounced with a "D" sound), is represented by the Yin Yang symbol, which is a half-white and half-black circle divided in a flowing motion down the center. The white half is associated with positivity, masculinity, and passivity, while the opposing black half represents negativity, femininity, and activity. In each side is one small circle of the opposing color, which symbolizes two main ideas: all things should be balanced and in harmony, and one side ultimately cannot exist without the other.

HISTORY

Lao Tzu is considered the founder of Taoism, though some people question his historical existence. Tradition holds that as an advisor to the Zhou Dynasty until age ninety, Lao Tzu was especially well-known for his wisdom in responding to questions about politics and religion.

As a contemporary of Confucius, Lao Tzu disagreed with many Confucian ideas. Lao Tzu believed Confucius was arrogant and idealistic. Lao Tzu believed that people were inherently good, and that there was no need to overcomplicate life with regulations. In fact, he felt that excessive involvement of government, religion, and other institutions would only heighten people's problems. Lao Tzu believed that the best way to maintain people's inherent goodness was for organizations and institutions to stay out of the way.

When Lao Tzu retired, many people encouraged him to write down his ideas. This suggestion resulted in the writing of the *Tao Te Ching*. Ironically, if Lao Tzu were alive today, he would likely be upset that anything he ever said was converted into a formal religious practice.

BASIC BELIEFS

The sacred text for Taoism is the *Tao Te Ching*, which was written in approximately 300 BCE. The writings in the *Tao Te Ching* are attributed to Lao Tzu, though there were probably many authors who contributed to the collection. The central purpose of the text is to guide its readers how to live in harmony with the universe.

Tao (the way) and Wu Wei (inaction) are two central concepts of Taoism. Some people consider Tao to be equivalent to the Christian concept of God, but that understanding is too concrete. No physical manifestations of the divine appear in the *Tao Te Ching*. A later text called *Zhuang Zi*, written by a lesser-known contributor by the same name, addresses ideas like immortality. An even later development in Taoism included personifications of the divine to provide an easier worship focus. These personifications are called the "Three Pure Ones." Regardless of these later developments, at the heart of Taoism remains the balance of all things.

To many Taoists, the beauty of Tao is in the mystery itself. Tao is the source of all being and nonbeing, the source of all energy in the universe. Tao is impersonal but omnipresent, and it has a movement, a flow with which Taoists seek to be in unity. There cannot be male without female, mountain without valley, or life without death. It is Tao that provides such balance, and it is the Taoist objective to be one with the flow, leading to the understanding of Wu Wei.

Wu Wei, inaction, is the universal basis for Taoist living. It is important to understand the difference between inaction and indifference. Wu Wei means that humans should allow Tao to do what Tao will do. Humans habitually want power and control, and this causes people to act in ways that are unnecessary. Nature will always return to a state of balance; humans must allow that to occur. Therefore, Wu Wei is not about being lazy and doing nothing; rather, it is about not interfering. Taoism would reject taking spontaneous action; instead, human action should always include ample time and consideration.

In addition to stressing peacefulness and balance in Wu Wei, Taoism also includes ancestor worship. This stems from the larger Chinese culture in which Taoism is embedded, as ancestor worship is a key feature of traditional Chinese religion. Most families have an ancestor altar at home where family members pray each day. This shrine typically has incense and a list of the deceased to be remembered. Historically, responsibility for the shrine fell to the eldest son.

DEMOGRAPHICS

Taoists rarely see conflict between following the Tao and being Buddhist. Thus, many Taoists claim more than one belief system. Some see themselves as followers of

both Confucianism and Taoism, despite the conflicts
between the founders. The idea is that each serves a
different purpose. It is even possible to practice Taoism
and Confucianism along with Buddhism or Shinto. There
are approximately 2.5 million Taoists worldwide, most of
whom are in China.

SHINTO

INTRODUCTION

The term *Shinto* means "the way of the kami (deities)," which comes from the Chinese language even though Shinto is indigenous to Japan. Shinto does not have a founder, a sacred text, a universal code of behavior, or a hierarchal leadership system in the traditional sense.

HISTORY

Shinto tradition dates to prehistoric times. We cannot trace the founding of Shinto to one person, and there is no written record recounting Shinto's beginnings, so we know very little about the origin of the tradition. However, there is a Shinto myth that tells of the creation of the Japanese Islands. There was always existence, and out of the kami came the world itself. The humanlike godor kami called Izanagi ("male") and Izanami ("female") were charged to create. The pair pierced a cosmic spear into the water, which created the first major Japanese land mass where Izanagi and Izanami lived. Together they created many kami. The last one born was the heat spirit, whose intensity burned through Izanami's uterus and killed her. She descended into the underworld. Izanagi went after her, but she positioned herself in the entrance of the underworld in order to stop him from entering in order to protect him. Enraged and filled with corruption and pollution, Izanagi returned to the earth. As he purified himself, the corruption in his left eye became the sun kami and his right eye the moon kami. The pollution he released from his nostrils created the kami of wind and storm.

During the sixth century, Shinto tradition underwent a process of formalization. Prior to this time, Shinto was so deeply embedded in Japanese culture that there was little need for definition. However, this changed when Buddhism spread from China into Japan, creating a need for Shinto practitioners to define themselves against non-Shinto traditions. Because competing traditions played a role in this formalization, these other traditions had a lasting influence on Shintoism. Some people believe that Shinto is partly Buddhism and partly Taoism; however, a more accurate statement is that Shinto is compatible with Buddhism and Taoism, allowing Shinto practitioners to assume more than one religious identity. Shinto has no creed and does not actively seek converts; most people are simply born into the religion. In Shinto there is no conflict in practicing more than one religion, so many Japanese people are both Buddhist and Shinto.

The emperor of Japan is a significant leader within Shinto because he serves as the official figurehead of the religion. However, today this is more of a ceremonial role, as the emperor does not make collective decisions or deliver doctrine in the same way that other religious leaders do. In the past, the emperor enjoyed great power among Shinto practitioners in Japan, as the people believed that the emperor himself was divine, and they worshiped him as such. However, after Japan was defeated in World War II, the role of the emperor decreased tremendously. People no longer worship the emperor as a deity, and although the emperor is still respected, there is less of a relationship between the government and Shinto today.

BELIEFS

Shinto is a polytheistic religion, as there is a belief in many kami who are omnipresent throughout the universe. Kami can take many forms in the natural world such as waterfalls, mountains, or flowers; kami can be present in human or animal forms; or they can choose to be formless. Shrines exist where people can worship the kami. Shrines are typically near some body of water, and most shrines are built in areas that are peaceful and natural. Shrines built in cities are usually surrounded by trees. There are no regular services held in Shinto tradition, so practitioners choose to visit shrines whenever they wish. At the shrine, people enter through a torii gate, often considered to be the symbol of the Shinto religion. The shrine itself is used to get the attention of the kami, and people use the area around the shrine for worship as well as the shrine itself. Because of this reverence for the natural world, Shinto practitioners frequently align themselves with environmental issues and promote conservation.

In Shinto, practitioners place great emphasis upon the idea of purity. Even before visiting a shrine, worshippers will be sure to bathe and dress in clean clothes. Upon arrival at the torii gate, they will wash their hands and feet again. In the Shinto worldview, people believe that human beings are born good, and over a lifetime humans become impure. Therefore, there are many priest-led rituals that focus on purification.

Home shrines called kamidana typically allow practitioners to worship ancestral spirits. Kamidana will often have small torii gates and be visually unadorned. There are no images at these shrines; however, practitioners often write down the names of deceased loved ones and then burn them. The family will leave offerings of flowers or food at the altar and will visit every day; without this daily visit, the kami may become upset.

DEMOGRAPHICS

There are approximately 3 million Shinto practitioners in the world, most of whom live in Japan. Shinto permits women to be priests, though there are still significantly fewer female than male priests. Shinto influenced the beginnings of two religious movements in Japan: Tenrikyo and Omoto. Both have female founders, began in the eithteenth century, and emphasize earthly personal restoration rather than preparation for the afterlife.

SHAMANISM

INTRODUCTION

Shamanism is not a religion. Rather, it is a practice seen in various indigenous traditions around the world. There are shamans not only in North and South American indigenous religions, but also in some African and Asian religions. For example, both Yoruba and Shinto traditions include this practice.

HISTORY

Archaeologists have traced the worldwide use of shamans in tribal religions back to over 25,000 years ago. Shamans are considered to be intermediaries between the physical and spiritual worlds. People believe that shamans have special abilities to communicate with animals and plants, can control the weather, and share prophesies through the use of chanting, dancing, and prayers. Shamans are also able to remove evil spirits from people and communities.

In order to become a shaman, a person must go through a rigorous process. Most shamans claim to be called by the spirit world to take on this role and go through a symbolic spiritual death and rebirth experience. For some shamans, the role is passed down through many generations in their families. There is typically a process of purification that requires intense fasting, isolation, and spiritual contact for a period of time.

BELIEFS

A shaman is a central leader in his or her community. Shamans can be either male or female and are often considered to be a combination of counselor, pastor, and physician; this complex role has led some people to identify shamans as "medicine men." Many shamans treat community illnesses and ailments by using natural remedies like herbs. People often go to shamans because they are looking for a healer to cure emotional, spiritual, or physical problems. Also, a person may visit a shaman if she is having problems conceiving, or if he or she wants to communicate with the spirit of an ancestor.

The shaman's responsibilities are based on the belief that he or she is in contact with the spirit world through dreams, trances, or visions. Consequently, shamans will sometimes use mind-altering substances like peyote, cannabis, or opium to bring about a state in which such dreams or visions are more likely to occur. Many shamanic rituals focus on divination, which involves viewing the future or revisiting the past. Sometimes shamans conduct ceremonies to communicate with ancestors or animal spirits on behalf of tribal communities seeking protection or rewards. Shamans have been known to identify themselves with natural elements like mountains or waterfalls, or sometimes with animal spirits. There is a common belief among indigenous religions that spirits inhabit the natural world. Communication with those spirits allows believers to stay connected to the earth.

DEMOGRAPHICS

It is nearly impossible to determine how many individuals worldwide practice Shamanism. However, the basic experiential practice of shamans has become more well-known to the Western world through the work of Professor Michael Harner, who has dedicated his life to the study of shamans. Harner believes that the West has been stripped of its shamanic or spiritual connection thanks to years of rejection of native traditions. Harner's goal is for all people to understand and accept the interconnectedness of the spirit world that is all around them.

FOR FURTHER READING

http://www.shamanism.org/index.php

CONFUCIANISM

INTRODUCTION

Confucianism does not have a hierarchy of leadership, central creed, or regular form of worship; nor does Confucianism require belief in any type of deity. As a result, is often considered to be more of a philosophy than a religion. However, Confucianism does include an ethical system of behavior which emphasizes honoring family, following rules, and appreciating the surrounding culture. Confucianism takes its name from its founder Confucius.

HISTORY

Confucius was born in China in 551 BCE. At that time, China was separated into various regions with different rulers. Confucius's father died when he was young, and his mother raised him in poverty, but Confucius was well educated. After the death of his mother, he became a teacher and later was hired to work for the government, based upon his wise reputation. During his life, Confucius also became a husband and father, and then finally he died in 479 BCE.

During Confucius's life, he encountered many conflicts in society, which ultimately led him to value the importance of social harmony. Confucius believed that all human beings were capable of good, and that with some guidance, people could achieve a peaceful community. Confucianism became a more formal religious system during the rise and spread of Buddhism in the first century CE. Buddhism emphasizes the rejection of attachment to the material world, which many Confucians feared would create a disregard for social responsibility. The belief that Buddhism would have a negative impact upon the larger community forced Confucians to organize their beliefs in order to ensure social harmony.

Later on, the scholar Zhu Xi contributed writings that addressed behavior and proper rituals, aiming to popularize Confucianism. For centuries afterward, Confucians had to memorize entire portions of his writings during exams. Zhu Xi's impact on Confucianism was as influential as that of Confucius himself.

BELIEFS

Confucianism is a system which governs how people interact with one another and the world around them. There are five great relationships which serve as a model for individual daily behavior, while five great virtues serve as a code to enrich the entire society. Confucian philosophies are embedded in the very fabric of Chinese culture and are considered to be indigenous Chinese ideology.

The five central relationships are father–son, elder brother–younger brother, husband–wife, old–young, ruler–subject. The father–son relationship refers to the parents' responsibility to instill moral values in a child, and in return the child should be respectful and obedient. The elder brother–younger brother relationship points out the need for the elder sibling to help guide the younger one through life as an extension of the parents. The elder son traditionally inherits all the paternal responsibility.

The husband–wife relationship is based on mutual care, but the husband still has authority over the wife. He is expected to be the financial provider and protector, while she is to be the homemaker. The old–young relationship (sometimes even thought to be a friend–friend relationship) is intended to foster loyalty and respect. The older person helps the younger in personal development, and the younger cares for the older as he or she ages. Finally, the ruler–subject relationship is a reflection of the social order both domestically and within the larger society. The ruler should protect and care for the subjects, but in return, the subject should be obedient to and supportive of the ruler. Loyalty is a key theme which is present in all five of these important relationships.

One of the most important aspects of Confucianism is a focus on social harmony. Confucians believe that there are five virtues that humans should promote, which will lead to social harmony: Ren, Li, Shu, Xiao, and Wen. Ren is benevolence or kindness. People should always have compassion and care for one another by exhibiting respect and politeness toward everyone with whom they interact. Li refers to proper behavior, which includes always following the laws of society. Shu would be most akin to the Golden Rule, meaning that a person should behave as he or she hopes to be treated in return. Aspects of Shu are apparent in the principle of Xiao, which refers to filial piety. Respect for all members of the family, past or present, is at the heart of Xiao. Not only should children honor their parents, but children should also care for their aging parents, and as adults, grown children should then have their own children who will respect, honor, and care for them. Finally, in the virtue of Wen, or culture, Confucius believed that people should take an interest in literature, art, and music. Believing that an appreciation for the arts would lead to more benevolent human interaction, Confucius referred to them as the "arts of peace." If all people followed these virtues, Confucius believed it would necessarily lead to a harmonious society.

The most well-known of the literature associated with Confucianism is *The I Ching* (the Book of Changes). *The I Ching* discusses the ideas of balance in the universe and the changing nature of existence.

DEMOGRAPHICS

Because the Communist regime in China has outlawed all religious practices, it is almost impossible to determine how many Confucians there are. Additionally, most Confucians also practice other religions such as Buddhism or Taoism alongside Confucianism. Therefore, many Confucians may not identify themselves as strictly practicing Confucianism.

ZOROASTRIANISM

INTRODUCTION

The ancient Persian religion Zoroastrianism is one of
the earliest monotheistic traditions, centered on the
one god Ahura Mazda. Zoroastrians believe in an all-
loving, benevolent god who allows people to have free
will. Humanity, not Ahura Mazda, causes evil to exist by
choosing to follow the evil spirit Ahriman, who opposes
Ahura Mazda. This is how Zoroastrians deal with the
problem of suffering with which many religions grapple.
Further, Zoroastrians believe that Ahura Mazda always
provides humanity with the opportunity for good and
gives human beings unwavering support in their spiritual
battle against evil.

HISTORY

Zoroastrianism is an ancient religion, as it began almost
3,500 years ago. The founder Zarathustra, or Zoroaster in
Greek, was a revolutionary of his time. In a culture that
was mostly polytheistic, Zarathustra emphatically rejected
polytheism and proclaimed his belief in only one god
named Ahura Mazda, or "Wise Lord." Zoroastrianism was
radically different from other religions of the time because
the purpose of Zarathustra's religion was not pleasing the
gods with sacrifices. Instead, Zarathustra believed that the
primary reason for religion was to have a personal ethical
system, which would ultimately situate humanity on the
side of goodness and truth.

The central text for Zoroastrians is the Avesta, likely written by Zarathustra. The Avesta originally contained seventeen gathas (hymns) that praise Ahura Mazda; however, today only fragments of the Avesta still exist. The writings in the Avesta make up what some people consider to be one of the greatest poetic collections in history, indicating that Zarathustra was probably well-educated; scholars believe that he also may have been a priest in the pre-Zoroastrian religion he so strongly criticized. However, there is little evidence of any specific educational training, for there are many unknowns about his life; even the time period of his existence is debated.

Zarathustra lived in what is now Iran. His religious proclamations were so radical that he and his followers were persecuted. As a result, Zarathustra fled to an area in modern-day Afghanistan. In this new land, the king of the region converted after Zarathustra miraculously healed the king's favorite horse. The king's support gave this new religion the political protection it needed to flourish.

As Zarathustra grew older, he began to emphasize the importance of marriage and family. In addition, Zarathustra encouraged people to work hard and to appreciate their lives.

BELIEFS

Zoroastrians believe in one almighty, wise creator being called Ahura Mazda, who is omnipotent, omniscient, and benevolent. Ahura Mazda created the world and humanity, and is the source of love and happiness. Having an absolute, unchanging moral character, Ahura Mazda is the guardian of all people. This is represented in the

Faravahar or Farohar, the symbol of Zoroastrianism. The birdlike Faravahar has at its center a human figure representing the human soul within the physical world, and this human is encircled by a ring that represents the immortality of the spiritual world. The wings on either side of the ring are lined with three rows of feathers, which represent good thoughts, good words, and good deeds—the three principles by which all Zoroastrians should try to live. The three rows of feathers on the tail likewise represent bad thoughts, bad words, and bad deeds, which humanity should always strive to avoid. Finally, the two lines which extend outward in opposite directions at the base of the figure represent the opposing forces of good and evil, between which humans must constantly choose.

When Ahura Mazda created humanity, he did not limit free will. According to Zoroastrians, humans have the opportunity to choose between good and evil; this choice is important because the universe is engaged in a cosmic battle between good and evil, and humans must fight on one side or the other. Before creation, there were twin spirits of good and evil. Spenta Mainya is the spirit of truth, and Angra Mainyu is the spirit of lie. The constant conflict between truth and lies manages all of humanity. This system of good versus evil is dualistic, meaning two forces are in opposition. While Ahura Mazda is the benevolent, supreme god, there is also an evil supernatural being called Ahriman, who functions very much like Satan in Christianity. Ahriman is called the "Father of Lies," and his job is to tempt humanity away from fighting on behalf of good.

Zoroastrians aim to live according to a modest doctrine of humata, hukhta and huveshta. Humata means "good thoughts," and these good thoughts should lead to hukhta, "good words." In turn, good words should be put into practice by doing huveshta, "good works." By unifying one's thoughts, speech, and actions under Ahura Mazda, Zoroastrians may live in harmony.

Zarathustra believed there were two possible fates for a person in the afterlife. A person either joins Ahura Mazda in pure joy in a heaven-like place, or the person is sent into Ahriman's hell-like pit of fire as a result of bad behavior. Significantly, Zoroastrians also look for a day of final judgment during which Ahura Mazda will finally conquer Ahriman, and good will ultimately triumph over evil. At this time, the dead will be resurrected, and all those who were faithful will live forever with Ahura Mazda in this newly renovated, perfect paradise.

Worship is usually an individual practice rather than being communal, but there are also several rituals and festivals that are celebrated as a community. Zoroastrian places of worship are called Fire Temples because they always contain a sacred fire as a symbol of Ahura Mazda. Many Zoroastrian homes have small fire altars for domestic worship; the sacred flame must always remain burning both at home and in the temple, a practice which stretches back into ancient times.

DEMOGRAPHICS

There are approximately 200,000 Zoroastrians in the world today. The largest populations are found in Northern India, Pakistan, and Iran. The number of

Zoroastrians has decreased significantly over time. One reason for this decrease is Zoroastrianism's refusal to accept converts into the religion. Additionally, the rise of Christianity and Islam and their political power over Zoroastrian regions caused a decline in the number of Zoroastrians. Nevertheless, Zoroastrians live in countries all over the world.

RASTAFARIANISM

INTRODUCTION

Colonization of the Caribbean by white Europeans and their subsequent enslavement of Africans planted the seed for the religion of Rastafarianism. This religion focuses upon the desire to restore an African homeland, specifically the promised land of Ethiopia. As a monotheistic religion, Rastafarianism draws upon many influences in Christianity and Judaism.

HISTORY

In the 1930s, a Jamaican named Marcus Garvey started the Universal Negro Improvement Association, which aimed to return all people of African descent to their places of origin. Garvey believed that the crowning of the Ethiopian emperor Haile Selassie was the beginning of the fulfillment of this prophecy; therefore, Garvey considered him to be a messiah. In fact, the word "Rastafarianism" is based on Selassie's title and name before becoming emperor (Ras Tafari).

Race is a significant issue in Rastafarianism. Leonard Howell, an early leader of the Rastafari movement, proclaimed six major doctrinal beliefs, two of which were opposition to the white culture which engendered slavery, and God's actions of justice and revenge against this culture. Howell also promoted the superiority of black culture in an effort to shed a long history of oppression. Howell was briefly jailed by the Jamaican government on the charge of sedition, primarily due to his devotion to Selassie. Afterward, the Rastafarian movement intentionally remained without a formal leader.

In 1966, Haile Selassie visited Jamaica, which was a monumental event. Rastas understand this visit to be the beginning of the liberation they seek, giving them hope for an ultimate return to Ethiopia, the promised land.

BELIEFS

Rastas believe in one true god called Jah, who is within all people. Through meditation and experience, Jah bestows personal revelations upon those who are faithful. Rastas believe that Africans are descended from the Israelites, and that they were sent into exile because of the color of their skin. According to Rastafarian tradition, Ethiopia is connected to Israel through the son of King Solomon and the Queen of Sheba. This is why Ethiopia is considered to be the promised land, and Babylon is the physical representation of hell. This relationship to the Israelites allows the Rastas to believe in a legacy of prophets beginning with Moses.

Rastas believed that Haile Selassie was Jah in human form—the King Divine, who proclaimed that death would only affect the unrighteous. Rastas also believe in reincarnation, and that one's same identity will be maintained in subsequent lives.

One important ritual in Rastafarianism is the "reasoning session." Traditionally practiced only by males, reasoning sessions are opportunities for people to gather and to share their goals with one another. The group will use marijuana as a holy herb that is a source of nutrition, spiritual revelation, and relaxation. This practice is not obligatory, although most Rastafarian men do participate.

Rastafarianism is a patriarchal religion. As noted above, women do not take part in "reasoning sessions," and historically women's roles in Rastafarianism have been restricted to domestic life, while men assume spiritual responsibilities. Early in the religion's history, men often addressed women as daughters, regardless of age, though in recent years men have begun referring to women as Queens. The Queen's objective is to care for the King (her husband), who is the head of household. There are also prohibitions against birth control and abortion, and women are considered unclean during menstruation.

Many Rastafarians wear dreadlocks, imitating the appearance of Old Testament warriors who were lost in the wilderness. Rastas believe it was strength from Jah, the Lion of Judah, which helped the warriors survive. Dreadlocks are also a symbol of political protest. When slaves were transported from Africa to the European colonies, upon arrival slave owners shaved the Africans' heads. Thus, wearing dreadlocks is seen as an outward rejection of persecution.

THE ORISHA TRADITIONS

INTRODUCTION

Orisha religion is simultaneously indigenous and modern, forming the basis of West African native religion as well as a number of unique modern traditions in the Americas. The Orisha tradition originated in West Africa and then traveled to the Western world through the slave trade. Attempts at forced conversion by Christian slave owners resulted in Orisha traditions changing and evolving once Africans were transplanted to European colonies. Orisha traditions are often labeled religions of the oppressed because of the many changes that resulted from the slave trade, both in the Yoruba homeland and in the colonies.

Believing that Orisha traditions were based on superstition, European colonists called these practices devilish and even dangerous because believers practiced in secrecy. This secrecy caused suspicion, which led to misunderstandings about the Orisha traditions that have continued into the present day. Popular culture has contributed to this misunderstanding because movies, television, and books often misrepresent Orisha religion as superstitious and demonic.

HISTORY

The Orisha tradition began in Nigeria within the Yoruba culture. Though some people might misinterpret this religion as polytheistic because of the multiple Orisha (spirits), Yoruba religion is actually henotheistic—worshipping only one god among many. The Orisha are spirits typically associated with natural elements like the harvest, the sky, or the sea. These Orisha are the intermediaries between humans and the one genderless, formless, omnipotent god, called Olodumare.

Beginning in the sixteenth century, European slave traders transported many Yoruba men, women, and children to the Americas, which were predominantly Christian. In this unfamiliar land, slave owners attempted to force Christianity upon their slaves, who quickly adapted their own religious practices in order to make it appear that they had converted to Christianity. These adaptations led to the birth of several hybrid Orisha traditions, which combine Yoruba religion with Catholicism. The most well-known of these traditions are Vodou (Haiti) and Santeria (Cuba).

BELIEFS

Although the names of the spirits are not alike, the core of the Orisha traditions is the same. They worship one omnipotent and omniscient prime mover who is disconnected from humanity. With the assistance of spirits, believers can find peace, redemption, understanding of their destinies, communication with the deceased, and healing. In Orisha traditions, dancing and drumming are important aspects of rituals, as these are the ways for humans to communicate with the Orisha and to invite them to be physically present among humanity. Divination is also central to Orisha traditions; with the help of a priest (*babalawo*), a person can use divination to communicate with the Orisha and receive guidance and healing.

Santeria

Santeria, "the way of the saints," is primarily in Cuba, just ninety miles south of the United States. Santeria has no specific governing body. Each priest (*santero*) operates his own *casa de santos*, or house of the saints. The *casa de santos* is not a formal church or temple, but rather a home that is used for worship and ritual. There is no central leadership and no unified doctrine, though *santeros* do consult with high priests, called *babalawos*. The *babalawo* is believed to have a direct line of communication with the Orisha, while the Orisha communicate with Olodumare.

Each practitioner has a specific Orisha to whom he or she prays. In Santeria, instead of praying in a position of reverence, people prefer to pray face-to-face with the Orisha using images of Catholic saints. For example, Saint Barbara is used to worship the Chango, whose domain is the storm. This association stems from Saint Barbara's identity as the patron saint of the military, and a popular story about her involves lightning striking her father when he tried to kill her. Each Orisha has a specific holiday to be celebrated and a feast day to be observed. In addition, each Orisha has specific rituals that are conducted in his or her honor.

Some critics believe that Santeria hides within the boundaries of Catholicism, but believers insist that they are both Catholic and Santeria at the same time, seeing no conflict between the two because they see many avenues to reach the same true god. However, papal Catholic tradition would disagree and say that Santeria cannot be practiced legitimately alongside Catholicism.

In order to become a follower of Santeria, a person must seek out a *santero* and then undergo a series of initiation rituals. At the conclusion of the first ritual, the initiate learns the identity of the Orisha to whom he or she will pray, and is also given a necklace that will protect against evil. The main goal of Santeria is to achieve harmony with the spiritual and physical realms.

Santeria has no central written text. Instead, there is ancient Yoruba oral tradition that has been passed down to the present. This oral collection is called the *Corpus of Ifa*. Each individual also has a personal notebook called a *liberta* that is a gift from his or her *padrino*, or godfather. The *liberta* contains handwritten rituals, practices, advice, and incantations for divination. The *liberta* is different for every person.

Vodou

Vodou means "the mysterious force," and has similar West African roots to Santeria. The African slaves who were transported to Haiti were baptized by Catholic priests as soon as they arrived at the island. The result was not conversion to devout Catholicism, but rather a move to practice native religion in secret. This secrecy has led to great speculation, causing many misconceptions of Vodou.

Like Santeria, Vodou has a genderless, omnipotent god who is not present in this world. This god is called Bondyé, derived from the French phrase *Bon Dieu*, literally "Good God." There are also spirits called the Loa to whom believers pray. The Loa each have unique domains, including the sea, storm, war, creation, love, and more. Like Santeria, Vodou's Loa have connections to Catholic saints, and these spirits do interact with people on earth. Additionally, each Loa has specific prayers, dances, and festivals associated with him or her, and people come to individual Loa with specific prayers, requests, and questions.

Vodou ritual is typically practiced in homes of priests (*houngans*) or priestesses (*mambos*). A common focus of worship is healing, which is a vital aspect of practically all Vodou ritual. Vodouisants also perform rituals to claim lost ancestor souls, since unclaimed souls in the afterworld can be dangerous for those still living. These souls can cause unrest, but if they are respected, no harm will come to the living.

DEMOGRAPHICS

Yoruba religion is still alive and well in Nigeria, Togo, and Benin. Over 60 million people, mostly in the Americas, practice Vodou. There are also other Orisha traditions with roots in Yoruba religion, including Candomble in Brazil and Shango in Trinidad. There are over 100 million practitioners in Brazil; 5 million people practice Santeria between Cuba and the United States.

NEOPAGANISM, WICCA, AND DRUIDISM

INTRODUCTION

Neopaganism refers to a group of religions that draws beliefs and practices from ancient nature-based traditions. For many people, the term *pagan* is used derogatorily to insinuate someone is going against the norm or is uncivilized. The original meaning of the term comes from the Latin *pagus*, which typically refers to a piece of land or countryside. Thus, the word *paganus* referred to those country folk who held onto ancient religious practices and refused to convert to Christianity.

Some of the most well-known Neopagan traditions are Wicca and Druidism, though there are many traditions which make up paganism overall. Ancient Roman, Greek, and Egyptian religions are examples of ancient pagan traditions. Ancient Chinese traditions that focus on the earth and spirits have also been categorized as pagan faiths.

HISTORY

The religious traditions of Neopaganism stretch back into antiquity, so there is no primary founder or originating group. Throughout history, these religions have been persecuted as heretical under Christian and Islamic rule. However, in recent years, the number of Neopagan practitioners has been on the rise. Such an increase could be the result of global concerns about climate change or diminishing natural resources, as these ancient traditions promote a spiritual connection to the earth. Regardless, over the last fifty years, groups like Pagan Pride have developed in support of these religious traditions.

BELIEFS

Wicca

Within the Wiccan religion, there are many different beliefs. Some Wiccans believe there are many gods, while others believe in only one. Some focus on the concept of a dual-gendered deity having both male and female characteristics, whereas others emphasize only the feminine and therefore engage in goddess worship.

Most holidays center on seasonal changes. There are a total of eight high holy days called Sabbats, which fall upon solstices and equinoxes. On the monthly occurrence of the full moon, called Esbat, there is usually a communal service. The pentacle, or pentagram, is the most well-known Wiccan symbol. Each point represents an element: earth, air, water, fire, and spirit. Spirit is considered the most important element of the natural world. Wiccan practitioners are traditionally called witches, whether male or female, and the practice of Wicca is called witchcraft. There is no central sacred text for Wiccans, but many covens (groups of Wiccans) will collect incantations (spells or prayers used in ceremonies) to pass down from generation to generation. Wiccans believe that they may behave in any way they choose as long as it harms no other person. This ethic is called the Wiccan Rede.

Druidism

Druidism is the second largest Neopagan tradition, with the largest number of practitioners in England. Druidism began in the eighteenth century, and Druids suffered great persecution for their beliefs. Druidism's connection to ancient nature-based religion is not as evident as in Wicca, but many Druids do trace their faith back to the ancient Celts as far as 4,000 BCE. Druids are mostly polytheistic, claiming approximately thirty primary deities and several other less significant deities as their pantheon. Most of these deities are related to nature, with the sun god and fire god being the most important. While many Druids are polytheistic, some Druids are monotheists, and still others are animists. Druid worship is traditionally in orchards filled with oak trees, which is why the term Druid means "oak tree wisdom." Holy days, also called Fire Festivals, are associated with season changes. Druids have four high holy days, with each falling between solstice and equinox. The Druid belief system is very open, and not every Druid practices in the same way. Druids hold respect for nature and promote peaceful human interaction.

DEMOGRAPHICS

There is no current worldwide estimate of how many people are Neopagans. However, Adherents.com claims that there are approximately one million practitioners as of the year 2000. That number has most likely grown over the last eleven years. Because there are so many religions that may or may not be classified as Neopagan, accurate estimates are impossible to attain. The largest number of Wiccan practitioners is in the United States.

NATIVE AMERICAN RELIGION

INTRODUCTION

Though all Native American traditions are not the same, with each tribe having its own unique beliefs and practices, there are still some common elements. Native American religious traditions differ from many other religions because, like most indigenous religions, their spiritual practices are enmeshed within tribal culture as a way of life.

HISTORY

Native American tribes felt a great impact on their way of life during the European colonization of North and South America beginning in the fifteenth century. Tribes suffered and died from the introduction of new illnesses from which Native Americans had no immunity, and native peoples lost their lands as European settlers forced them from their traditional homes. Because tribal ceremonies often had strong ties to the land, loss of this land necessitated many changes to the ways that tribes worshiped. Tribes were decimated as they fought back against settlers. Christian missionaries either forced conversion upon Native Americans or encouraged syncretistic practice, which means that tribes blended their own spiritual traditions with Christian practices. In 1887, the United States government passed the Dawes Act, which outlawed all Native American expressions of religion, and this policy stayed in place for nearly fifty years. During this time, Native Americans were unable to practice religious ceremonies or wear traditional tribal dress without fear of punishment by authorities. Relationships between Native Americans and the surrounding culture continue to be complicated by this difficult history.

BELIEFS

Most tribes do not have written scriptures or doctrinal beliefs; traditions have survived by oral transmission over the course of many years. During the colonial period, many Native Americans believed that oral tradition was safer because European settlers would not be able to destroy tribal beliefs if they had been committed to memory. Only very recently have some tribes begun to transcribe some of their beliefs in written form for future generations.

Tribal religious traditions vary in terms of their development and history. Many Native American tribes believe that their ancestors have always been on the same land for as far back as time can go. Consequently, numerous beliefs and rituals are geographically centralized. Beliefs are focused on the sacredness of the natural world and reverence for ancestors. Many Native American traditions are considered to be pantheistic, meaning that the divine is in all things in the natural world, including mountains, plants, animals, trees, etc. However, some tribes do believe in a divine creator and offer prayers to this deity as the creator god. Some tribes also honor a wider pantheon of deities who govern different aspects of the natural world.

Shamans, sometimes called medicine men, serve as physical and spiritual leaders of a tribe. Shamans will prescribe traditional natural remedies for people suffering from illnesses. The Shaman is also considered to be the primary communicator with the divine, and thus is the leader of ceremonial rituals, which typically include drumming, chanting, and dancing. There are many specific occasions for these rituals like coming of age, purifying people or objects, honoring the ancestors, and giving thanks to the land. Some tribes may use substances such as marijuana, tobacco, or peyote for ceremonial practices. Ceremonies can be public or private, though most are closed to nontribal members.

DEMOGRAPHICS

There are approximately 250,000 Native Americans in the United States. This population was significantly reduced due to colonization, which at times has been described as genocide. Over time, many Native Americans have converted to other religions, so the number of people practicing tribal spiritual traditions is lower than the total population of Native Americans in the United States.

RELIGIONS OF PLACE COMPARED TO CHRISTIANITY

	NATURE OF GOD	NATURE OF HUMANITY	NATURE OF THE UNIVERSE	NATURE OF RELIGION	FOUNDERS AND TEXTS
CHRISTIANITY	One creator-God in three persons: Father, Son, and Holy Spirit. God is personal, interacts with humanity, is all-knowing, and all-powerful.	God allows humans free will to choose between right and wrong. However, they are inherently sinful and are incapable of achieving salvation on their own. Ultimately, salvation only comes through God.	This world is temporary. We are engaged in a battle between good and evil. Someday God will judge all people at the end of time, which will bring the long-awaited coming of the "Kingdom of God."	Through belief in Jesus Christ, humans are saved from sin and will have eternal life after death. Because Jesus is the supreme sacrifice to atone for the sins of humanity, Christianity is the only path to salvation.	The founders were followers of Jesus of Nazareth, born sometime between 7 BCE and 1 CE. Texts include the Bible (including Old and New Testaments) and, for some Christians, the Apocrypha.
TAOISM	Taoist beliefs vary; some Taoists worship a variety of deities, spirits, and/or ancestors, while others simply observe a reverence for the Tao, or "the Way," which represents the nature of the universe.	Humans have a dual nature, with the body representing both spiritual principles and the natural world. In achieving spiritual balance, one aligns oneself with nature and moves into harmony with the Tao, which should be the goal of all humankind.	The universe is animated by qi, the life force which flows through everything, and is ordered by Tao. The balance of the universe is captured in the Yin Yang symbol, showing the interdependence of opposites; both sides are necessary to achieve harmony.	Taosim advocates compassion, moderation, and humility. Religion should move people to moral action and should teach restraint and self-control, ultimately bringing people into balance with nature and the universe.	Founder Lao Tzu may have lived in the 6th century BCE, though scholars question his historical existence. He is credited with writing the *Tao Te Ching*, the most prominent text in Taoism. There are also many secondary texts.
SHINTO	Deities or spirits called kami are present throughout the natural world. Kami may take forms or be formless. They can grant blessings or deliver curses, and people worship them at shrines throughout Japan.	Human beings are spirits who inhabit bodies, though human spirits differ from kami spirits. If people live moral lives, they may become ancestral spirits after death.	The Shinto universe is restricted to the Japanese islands, which are divine in origin. The people, land, and spirits of Japan are all intimately connected to one another.	Shinto is a collection of beliefs and practices that connects people to Japanese history, culture, and geography. Though it includes shared spirits, myths, and rituals, Shinto is better defined by action than belief.	As an ancient religion that dates back to prehistoric times, Shinto has neither a single founder nor any sacred texts.

	NATURE OF GOD	NATURE OF HUMANITY	NATURE OF THE UNIVERSE	NATURE OF RELIGION	FOUNDERS AND TEXTS
SHAMANISM	Shamanism involves a belief in spirits, which may or may not exist alongside any deities.	Though the world is full of spiritual beings, most humans are unable to see them or communicate with them, with the exceptions of shamans.	There are multiple planes of existence: the human world, and the spiritual world. Shamans are able to pass between these two realities, serving as mediums between humans and spirits.	Shamans communicate with spirits and/or ancestors in the past, present, or future. These spirits offer guidance, cure physical or spiritual illnesses, and bestow protection upon people.	Shamanism spans multiple belief systems, so there is no single text or founder.
CONFUCIANISM	Confucianism does not include belief in a specific deity.	All people are capable of being good and, with guidance, achieving social peace and harmony, as long as they treat one another with kindness and respect.	Though there is no specific deity, there is still reverence for (and in some cases, worship of) ancestral spirits. The ethical code of Confucianism honors the ancestors' expectations.	Using social relationships as models to establish ethical values, people may achieve an ideal society. Confucianism is not an other-worldly religion; rather, its focus is on humane actions and obligations in this life, within the material world.	Confucius, born in 551 BCE, founded Confucianism. The most important text is the ancient Chinese text called the I Ching, which dates prior to 2000 BCE, long before Confucius ever lived.

RELIGIONS OF PLACE COMPARED TO CHRISTIANITY *continued*

	NATURE OF GOD	NATURE OF HUMANITY	NATURE OF THE UNIVERSE	NATURE OF RELIGION	FOUNDERS AND TEXTS
ZOROASTRIANISM	One uncreated God (Ahura Mazda) who embodies absolute goodness, and who rivals a similarly singular, uncreated evil force (Ahriman).	Humans are warriors in the cosmic battle between order and chaos, good and evil. Though Ahriman tries to tempt them away from goodness, people should resist and fight for goodness. Those who fight for good will go to heaven, and for evil will go to hell.	The physical world is temporary, and the spiritual is eternal. The world is a battleground between Ahura Mazda and Ahriman. Their fight will continue until the final day of judgment, when good will finally defeat evil, all will be judged, and the dead will be resurrected.	Good thoughts, good words, and good deeds bring people closer to Ahura Mazda. Fire is an important symbol of purity and divinity, and is present in most rituals. People look for a future savior (Saoshyant) to bring the renovation of the world in the final judgment.	No one knows exactly when the founder Zarathustra, or Zoroaster in Greek, lived; estimates stretch as far back as 6000 BCE. The Avesta is the most sacred text, of which only fragments still remain.
RASTAFARIANISM	One singular God named Jah, which Rastas identify with the Christian God. Some Rastas see Haile Selassie I, the emperor of Ethiopia from 1930 to 1974, as an incarnation of Jah, but others view Selassie simply as a messenger.	Rastas believe Africans are descended from the Israelites and remain Jah's chosen people. Some Rastas may be reborn into new bodies with the same identity, and others believe their present bodies can live forever.	*Babylon* is used to describe the modern world, which is evil and corrupt. Rastas look for future deliverance from bondage and freedom in the promised land of Ethiopia.	Rastas see their movement as an extension of Christianity, with Selassie as a modern messiah figure. While they hope for heavenly paradise someday, Rastas see this paradise as manifested on earth, in Ethiopia.	Though Selassie is the closest thing to a founder, he never explicitly embraced this role. In addition to the Christian Bible, many Rastas also consider the *Kebra Nagast* (dating back to the 13th or 14th century CE) to be sacred.

	NATURE OF GOD	NATURE OF HUMANITY	NATURE OF THE UNIVERSE	NATURE OF RELIGION	FOUNDERS AND TEXTS
ORISHA TRADITIONS	God is impersonal and unknowable; therefore, supernatural spirits (Orisha in Yoruba and Santeria, Loa in Vodou) serve as intermediaries between God and humanity.	Humans choose to support either ordering or chaotic forces, and are judged by God for their actions. Upon death, a good person may become an ancestral spirit, or choose to be reincarnated within the same family.	The universe has both material and spiritual realms that are in tension with one another. Humans are one type of being that exist alongside Orisha/Loa, ancestors, and demonic spirits.	Religion (prayer, sacrifice, communication with the Orisha) helps a person look inward and achieve spiritual transcendence. Through divination, a person may receive guidance to help battle chaos on both large and small scales.	Yoruba religion was founded by Orunmila, who lived around 3000 BCE. Vodou and Santeria are syncretistic religions and have no founders, though practitioners may use the Christian Bible as a sacred text.
NEO-PAGAN/WICCA/DRUID	No particular deity is affiliated with these traditions overall, though individual sects may worship certain deities.	Generally, people in these traditions attempt to do no harm to others. Specific views of humanity are unique to particular groups.	These traditions tend to be focused on the sacredness of the natural world.	Religious belief and ritual enhance a person's connection to nature and the life-force within it. Particulars vary among traditions.	These traditions have roots in antiquity and as such have no individual founders. Sacred texts are unique to individual groups and sects.

RELIGIONS OF PLACE COMPARED TO CHRISTIANITY *continued*

	NATURE OF GOD	NATURE OF HUMANITY	NATURE OF THE UNIVERSE	NATURE OF RELIGION	FOUNDERS AND TEXTS
NATIVE AMERICAN	Varies according to tradition. There are many deities and spirits among Native American religions.	Humans have soul-spirits like animals and other natural elements. Many tribes focus on respectful interactions between human and non-human souls, though details vary according to specific tribe.	Traditionally, the spiritual universe was tied to the particular ancestral land of each specific tribe. Reverence for the natural world is a common Native American feature.	Religious ritual focuses on honoring deities or spirits, restoring balance to nature, achieving purification, and/or seeking help from the divine. Specifics vary among tribes.	As indigenous traditions, Native American religions have no specific founders or texts. However, in many tribes, traditions have been passed down orally through the generations and serve the same function as a sacred text.

UNIQUELY AMERICAN RELIGIONS

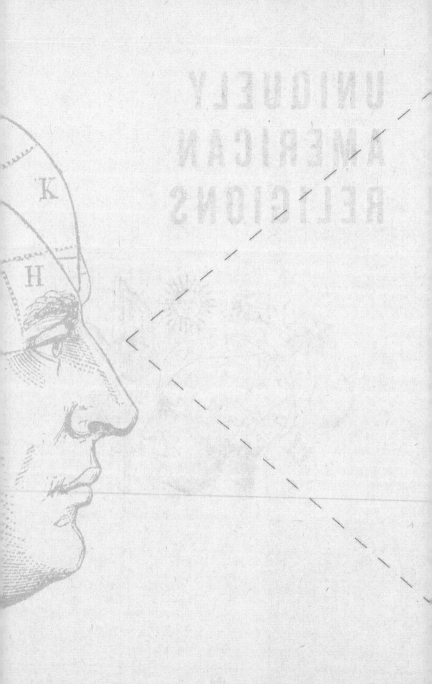

Mormonism

INTRODUCTION

Mormonism was founded in the United States during the 1800s. Also known as The Church of Jesus Christ of Latter-day Saints (LDS), Mormonism has endured religious persecution, undergone shifts in central doctrines, and spread globally through the church's missionary program. Whereas most Mormons would claim to be a part of the Christian tradition, many mainstream Christians would deny this claim because of Mormon beliefs about the trinity, the afterlife, and the Book of Mormon.

HISTORY

During the nineteenth century, Joseph Smith founded the Latter Day Saints movement. According to tradition, while living in New York, Smith found several gold plates that contained writings by the prophet Mormon. Smith claimed that God granted him the ability to translate and interpret the plates, which he called the Book of Mormon. Today, The Church of Jesus Christ of Latter-day Saints uses this collection of writings alongside the Old and New Testaments. Mormons consider the Book of Mormon to be the direct word of God.

Smith began the church in Kirtland, Ohio, where many people converted and began to establish the community of believers in the new Zion. Smith believed that God called him to establish the new promised land in the United States, and he oversaw the building of a temple to symbolize the sacred community bond; however, non-Mormons in the area began to disapprove of the expansion. Tensions were so high that these early Latter Day Saints moved to Nauvoo, Missouri.

The Latter Day Saints community built another temple in Missouri, and the community once again gained strength. Joseph Smith announced his candidacy for president of the United States in 1844, but shortly afterward, he and his brother were both assassinated. Shortly before Smith's assassination, he established a governing body of the church called the Quorum. The Quorum included twelve apostles, one of whom was Brigham Young.

After the assassination of Smith, Brigham Young immediately faced opposition from the non-Mormon community and believed it was important to avoid conflict; therefore, he once again relocated the community, this time to Utah. In Utah, Young established a theocracy, holding authority in both the church and government. Thirty years after the community moved to Utah, the settlers began to build the Tabernacle as a center for Mormon worship. Over time, the community suffered from both internal and external conflict, resulting from controversial issues like the practice of polygamy. In 1890, the federal government seized all of the church's assets. By this time, Joseph F. Smith was leading the community. Smith went before the United States Congress and publicly opposed the practice of plural marriage, and to this day,

The Church of Jesus Christ of Latter-day Saints officially rejects the practice of plural marriage.

BELIEFS

Members of The Church of Jesus Christ of Latter-day Saints view themselves as Protestant Christians. However, there are several Mormon beliefs that differ from other Christian denominations.

Mormons believe that the early Christian Church was corrupt, so they reject both the Nicene Creed and traditional concept of the trinity (Father, Son, and Holy Spirit). Whereas mainstream Christians believe that the trinity is three forms of the same divine essence, the LDS church believes that each form possesses its own divinity. Some Mormons believe that the Father was once in physical form and had sexual relations with Mary to conceive Jesus.

Though Mormons are unique in their belief that Jesus was married, they also share the common Christian belief that Jesus died for the sins of humanity, with acceptance and atonement resulting in the forgiveness of sins. The Book of Mormon claims that Jesus came to the Americas after he was crucified, buried, and resurrected. In contrast, no other Christian denomination believes that Jesus came to North and South America to share the gospel and perform miracles of healing. According to the Book of Mormon, the people of the Americas lived in perfect peace for more than 200 years after Jesus appeared to them.

Mormons believe that all souls have always existed; thus, they are not created. This is also unique to the

LDS church because most Christians believe that each individual soul is created by God to live only one life. In addition, because Mormons believe that God evolved from human form, they also believe that all Mormons can evolve into gods. For Christians, there is a distinction between humans and God, so there can be no moment of transformation into a divine being. The priesthood, or the community of Mormons, believes that non-Mormons can go to heaven, but they may not become gods.

The Church of Jesus Christ of Latter-day Saints considers the Book of Mormon to be the fifth gospel. Mormon tradition holds that a prophet by the name of Mormon collected the stories in ancient times and carved them into seven golden plates, which would later be found by Joseph Smith. The Book of Mormon relays an account of the ancient people of the Americas up through an account of Jesus's visit to North and South America. The book begins with the story of a man named Lehi, who was told by God to build a boat, take his family, and sail to the Americas. Lehi obeyed, so his family prospered.

Non-Mormons are not allowed to enter the Tabernacle or any other Mormon temple. Mormons consider the presence of a cross in sanctuaries to be idolatrous because they believe this is worship of a symbol in place of god. However, there are other widely used symbols, including the beehive and the seagull. The beehive is important not only because the early Mormons carried bees with them as they relocated to Utah, but also because the beehive symbolizes obedience to the word of god. Mormons ideally strive to work together, as does a hive of bees, with the result being the sweetness of social harmony. The seagull represents God's protection. Years ago, Mormon settlers in Utah found their crops attacked by locusts, and they feared they would have nothing to eat once their potential harvest was consumed. However, a flock of seagulls came through and devoured the locusts, thereby saving the crops. Mormons believe that the seagulls were a miracle sent by God.

A Mormon worship service always includes the celebration of communion, called the Sacrament, which consists of bread and water. Mormons are opposed to the use of wine or grape juice during the service. Other traditional Christian sacraments are observed but are not considered to be doctrinal. Baptism, conducted by full immersion, is considered to be an outward sign of a personal commitment to God, and baptism also admits a person into the priesthood of believers. Baptism is never performed before a child's eighth birthday because Mormons believe that someone should be able to understand the commitment he or she is making; therefore, Mormons do not believe in infant baptism. Only an adult authority in the priesthood of believers is allowed to perform baptisms.

Joseph Smith advocated several uniquely Mormon practices, including plural marriage, sealings, and baptism of the dead. Joseph Smith approved of polygamy, believing that this practice would expand the family of believers. He also believed that multiple wives could assist one another in household duties, though plural marriage was later abolished. Regarding marriage in general, Mormons do not believe that God recognizes civil marriages; therefore, a sealing ceremony is performed to ensure that husbands, wives, children, and extended families will remain together in the afterlife. Mormons also believe in baptism of the dead, giving the deceased another chance to gain entry into the kingdom of God. Usually conducted by a member of the priesthood, these baptisms require that another family member serve as the physical representative of the deceased during the ceremony.

Most Mormons also observe the Word of Wisdom, which Joseph Smith recorded as a revelation from God. The Word of Wisdom contains guidelines for Mormon behavior. For example, there are dietary regulations which encourage eating fruits and grains with only modest consumption of meat; there are also prohibitions against tobacco, alcohol, and caffeine. In addition, the Word of Wisdom encourages tithing a tenth of one's financial worth.

For many years, Mormons believed that dark skin was a physical representation of the legacy of Cain, from the biblical story of Cain and Abel. Since Cain killed Abel, the Mormons believed he was cursed by God. Therefore, dark-skinned people carried this association and were avoided by many Mormons. Only in 1978 were African-Americans permitted to become part of the priesthood of believers.

DEMOGRAPHICS

Within the United States, The Church of Jesus Christ of Latter-day Saints is the fourth largest Christian denomination, reaching almost 5.5 million members. However, most Mormons do not live in the United States; only twelve percent live in Utah, with the remaining eighty-eight percent scattered throughout the rest of the world.

Globally, the LDS church has made a great impact through its missionaries. Before young men marry, they typically go on a two-year mission trip to share their religious ideals and to help impoverished communities. This missionary impact is especially pronounced in Africa and Asia. In Africa, more than 250,000 people identify as Mormons, and in Asia, there are over 1 million Mormons. There are more than 14 million Mormons worldwide.

UNITARIAN UNIVERSALISM

INTRODUCTION

Unitarian Universalists consider themselves to be open-minded and welcoming to all people from all faiths at all times. However, many Christian denominations do not accept Unitarian Universalism as a branch of Christianity because they reject the doctrine of the trinity, and they recognize sacred traditions from multiple religions. Consequently, Unitarian Universalism is a marginalized group within Christianity overall.

HISTORY

During the Protestant Reformation in the sixteenth century, a group in Romania decided that the trinity had no scriptural basis. Based upon this belief, the group established the first Unitarian congregation, growing out of the Congregationalist movement. Early Unitarians were persecuted for questioning the ideas of the church, and for supporting the right of the individual to determine his or her own understanding of doctrine. In fact, the founder of Unitarianism in England, a scientist and theologian named Joseph Priestley, endured such vicious attacks in England that he eventually fled to the United States.

The very first Universalist Church of America was founded by Elhanan Winchester in New England in 1871. However, many similar groups around the United States developed at the same time. Early Universalists placed a heavy emphasis on evangelism. Additionally, because a core Universalist belief is that all human beings deserve dignity and respect, the first Universalists strongly supported social justice issues and spoke out against slavery.

Originally, there were two groups: the Unitarians, who proclaimed the unity of God and rejected Trinitarianism, and Universalists, who believed that all humans are saved. Both groups were on the fringe of more traditional Protestant churches, and in 1961, the two groups merged into one.

Both the Unitarians and the Universalists held open-mindedness and liberal philosophies to be important to their group identities.

BELIEFS

The central theme that unites all Unitarian Universalists is diversity. They believe that there is no one provable ultimate truth, and that there are multiple perspectives on spirituality and wisdom that contribute to personal development and spiritual growth. Unitarian Universalist worship services include writings from multiple religious traditions. Excerpts are drawn from texts like the *Dhammapada*, *Bhagavad Gita*, and the *Tao Te Ching*. Unitarian belief also incorporates a Judeo-Christian ethical understanding of being kind to one's neighbor, a humanist belief about the importance of reason, and perspectives on the natural world which are compatible with religious naturalism.

Sunday morning worship services resemble those of Protestant faith traditions. However, there are no official observances of sacraments like baptism, communion, or confirmation, and there is no central creed to follow. Most Unitarians also believe that Jesus was more of a social activist than the literal Son of God.

Many Unitarians would consider themselves monotheists in spite of their acceptance of multiple understandings of the divine. There are seven guiding principles for Unitarian Universalists:

1. Affirmation of the dignity and worth of all people.

2. Commitment to justice and compassionate action.

3. Support of each person's unique spiritual growth process, and acceptance of the differences that inevitably will exist.

4. Guarantee of freedom and responsibility in each individual's spiritual quest.

5. Commitment to the democratic process at all levels, from congregation to government.

6. Striving for global peace, freedom, and justice.

7. Maintaining respect for all life, including not only humans but extending throughout the natural world.

DEMOGRAPHICS

There are more than 1,000 churches with active membership, and approximately 250,000 Unitarian Universalists in the United States. Unitarian Universalists are fairly new to the religious landscape, which may explain their lack of a wider global presence; however, Canada and the U.S. Virgin Islands also report a significant population.

SCIENTOLOGY

INTRODUCTION

Scientology has encountered quite a bit of controversy since its founding. Some issues relate to conflicts with the United States' Internal Revenue Service. Also, many skeptics are suspicious of Scientology's seemingly secretive auditing practice.

Some people have accused the Church of Scientology of abuse through auditing. Many people question Scientology's status as a religion because of their financial gain through auditing fees charged to members (see below). In the early days of Scientology, the church struggled to gain religious organization status within the United States; therefore, it went to Europe to seek the same recognition, finally finding initial success in Great Britain. Additionally, the involvement of celebrities in Scientology appears to produce suspicion among the larger society. Recently, Tom Cruise has been highly criticized for his role in the Church of Scientology.

HISTORY

The Church of Scientology was established in 1954 by science fiction author L. Ron Hubbard. His father was a naval officer, so Hubbard had the rare opportunity to travel to Asia in 1927. Hubbard was highly influenced by Eastern religious thought and was also captivated by the works of Sigmund Freud. Scientologists believe that these two experiences deeply influenced Hubbard's book *Dianetics,* which was published in May of 1950 and remained on the New York Times best seller list for twenty-six weeks. Hubbard's motivation to write *Dianetics* was a result of his observations while working at an overseas medical facility during World War II. Hubbard noticed that the mental suffering of injured people inhibited their ability to recover and limited the effectiveness of medical interventions. In *Dianetics,* Hubbard explains his beliefs about human nature. Specifically, he describes how painful experiences of past lives are stored in what he calls the "reactive mind," and how these experiences lead to irrational behavior. He suggests that humans must rationally release the baggage of past lives in order to be happy.

BELIEFS

The central idea of Scientology is that human beings are spiritual souls who are trapped within their material bodies. Souls called thetans are immortal and continue from one material life to another collecting engrams, which are obstructions to the soul imprisoned by physical reality, or MEST (Matter Energy Space Time). These engrams manifest in a person's life as sadness, doubt, anger, or negative thoughts. A Scientologist's objective is to confront the engrams and release them, allowing the soul to live in a liberated state. Human beings are born with the potential to think rationally, and this ability is harnessed and applied to the process of removing engrams. Thetans are full of engrams from numerous past lives as well as their current lifetimes.

As the thetan moves toward full liberation from its engrams, it moves through a series of steps called the Bridge to Total Freedom, or Bridge, for short. Prior to the pursuit of the Bridge, a person is called a preclear, and once the Bridge is completed, the person becomes a clear or OT (Operating Thetan). The Bridge can be completed alone with the assistance of reading materials and specific techniques, but a preclear is strongly encouraged to have the assistance of a counselor, called an auditor. The auditor helps a person through the Bridge by asking reflection questions and using particular mental imagery to guide the preclear to recognize their engrams, which in turn removes them. An auditor may use a device called an e-meter, which is an electric machine designed to find engrams and help remove them from the preclear's thetan. There are fees charged for an auditing session at each stage of the Bridge. A person may exchange services to the church for auditing sessions, and sessions also can be conducted in group settings.

In the Scientologist creed, there is an emphasis on the concepts of equality, nonviolence, and spiritual sacredness, declaring that there are innate and unchallengeable rights that every human possesses. In addition, Scientologists believe that mental struggle should be addressed spiritually or religiously—not through exposure to the secular world. An individual who chooses to become part of the Church of Scientology would first be asked to enter a purification stage that would release all toxins from the body. This would be followed by an introductory course that explains the basic beliefs of the faith.

Scientologists believe that the practice of auditing can be followed alongside other religious traditions. Additionally, many Scientologists celebrate Christmas and Easter, not because of a belief in Jesus Christ, but because these holidays would be considered part of the cultural norm. Scientologists also have their own holidays; for example, March 13 is considered to be a holiday that celebrates the birth of L. Ron Hubbard. Most often worshippers will gather together in meeting rooms, and though most of the religious quest is done independently, there are communal services on Sundays. The meeting rooms are usually very modern and have multiple video displays with which members and visitors can interact. During services, readings or video clips from Hubbard are typically shared along with community announcements.

DEMOGRAPHICS

Scientology Centers (often called "churches") are located worldwide with members in 165 different countries.

Amish horse and carriage in Lancaster, PA

ANABAPTIST TRADITIONS

INTRODUCTION

The commitment to nonviolence is a unifying characteristic of the Mennonites, Amish, and Quakers among Christian Protestantism. The United States government has granted each of these denominations religious protection from obligatory wartimes, which was apparent during the Vietnam draft when members of these groups were excused from military service. In Anabaptist traditions, a peaceful way of life allows for simple, non-abundant living.

HISTORY/FOUNDERS

The Anabaptists were one of the many protest groups to form during the Christian Reformation, and they share many perspectives with other Protestant denominations, including the rejection of both transubstantiation and papal authority. However, Anabaptists have a unique belief regarding baptism. They believe that baptism should be performed only during adulthood, when the individual can understand the complexity of Christian belief, and that baptism can be performed over and over again. Whereas most Christian denominations believe in only one baptism, the Anabaptists believe that humans are highly fallible and thus are in need of the renewal, rebirth, and cleansing that baptism provides.

During the Reformation, an Anabaptist group formed in Switzerland under the leadership of Menno Simons, who professed a peaceful, nonviolent church philosophy. This group became known as the Mennonites. Though Mennonites are often thought to be a branch of conservative Christianity, they share many mainstream Christian beliefs.

Within the Mennonite community in 1693, a man named Jakob Ammann felt that the community was straying from its basic traditional beliefs. As a result, he began the Amish movement. All Amish are Mennonites, but not all Mennonites are Amish. Some people considered the Amish to be too extreme, often leading to persecution. This caused Amish groups to emigrate to other areas, including France, Germany, and eventually to America. Today in the United States, there are Amish communities in twenty-eight states, mostly located in the Midwest.

The Religious Society of Friends (also called the Quaker movement) was founded in England in 1647 by a preacher named George Fox. The Quakers believed deeply in the Christian call to nonviolence and felt that each Christian would personally receive "light" in the form of revelations from God. Thus, in the early days of the movement, Quakers were called the "Children of Light." Quakers do not have worship leaders because they believe that God will lead them spiritually. Quaker services, called meetings, typically involve a group of believers sitting silently together until someone is inspired by God to speak. Friends also reject the traditional Christian sacraments of communion and baptism, feeling that true communion lies in the gathering of believers rather than in the sharing of wine and bread, and that only the Holy Spirit can baptize. Later, Quakerism was established in Pennsylvania with the help of William Penn, who is also the state founder.

BELIEFS

Though these groups share the same belief system as the larger Christian church, there are also some differences in lifestyle and worship, which separate them from other Christians.

Mennonites believe deeply in the separation of church and state advocated by Jesus in the New Testament. They also believe in adult baptism and in the supremacy of the New Testament. As Anabaptists, they avoid becoming too involved in the material world; therefore, they try to limit their possessions, but they are not as extreme as the Amish. They also believe in peace and nonviolence with no exceptions. There are no churches because worship services are conducted in the home.

The Ordnung ("order") in the Amish community outlines the rules for Amish life. For example, the Ordnung prohibits gambling, wearing jewelry, using electricity, and owning televisions. The Ordnung also outlines the kind of clothing a person should wear, the type of buggy one should drive, and the language one should speak, which should be German or Swiss. Though the Amish lead a restricted lifestyle, youth in Amish communities traditionally undergo a period called Rumspringa, or "running around." This is a period of time during adolescence when the young person goes into the modern world and experiences life outside of the traditional community. Ideally, once the youth has experienced non-Amish life, he or she will ultimately choose to reenter the community through baptism, willingly committing to a life of simplicity. The extreme rejection of modernity is difficult, so Rumspringa makes this rejection a voluntary decision rather than an automatic requirement.

Above all, one of the most important Amish commitments is the rejection of Hochmut, which is a type of self-important pride. Hochmut goes hand in hand with humility, or Demut. As a demonstration of humility, Amish people do not pose for photographs. Members of the community who fall for the allure of modern life or who exhibit pride would likely be shunned by the community.

Most Amish only attend formal school provided by the community until the eighth grade. In 1972, the United States Supreme Court ruled that it was unconstitutional to require compulsory school attendance for the Amish until the age of 16, which is the mainstream American norm. After formal education is completed, Amish youth learn specific trades like farming or carpentry, which are skills that actively contribute to survival in the community.

Because the Amish way of life is completely voluntary, the community's rejection of traditional education and modern conveniences are ways of actively setting limits for itself. However, there are some reasonable exceptions to the Ordnung, based upon necessity. For example, some people may have telephones, though they would use them rarely, or a person may ride in a car to visit a distant family member or to attend a medical appointment in the city.

Unlike the Amish, who have many rules governing the community, Quakers do not have a central doctrine; therefore, it may seem to outsiders that they have no specific beliefs at all. However, since there is such an emphasis upon a personal relationship with God, it is difficult for a single creed to be applicable to all Friends; as a result, each person's specific beliefs are unique. In spite of this fact, there are some unifying features of Quakerism, like the dedication to nonviolence and the focus on individual religious experience.

DEMOGRAPHICS

The Mennonites, the Amish, and the Quakers are primarily located in the United States. However, these groups are present across the globe. There are approximately 350,000 Quakers worldwide. There are one million Amish in North America, about 250,000 of whom are in Pennsylvania. Mennonites exist in small groups across the world and total about 1.5 million.

INTRODUCTION

The Nation of Islam (NOI) is a separatist religious sect, founded in the United States in the 1930s, whose followers are primarily of African-American descent. While the Nation of Islam has many similarities to orthodox Islam, such as a belief in one God and the authority of the prophet Muhammad, the Nation of Islam also has distinct beliefs that have put them in conflict with greater Islam. Today, the Nation of Islam is led by the Honorable Minister Louis Farrakhan and has nearly 30,000 members, plus thousands more additional sympathizers.

HISTORY

The Nation of Islam began in Detroit, Michigan under the leadership of Wallace Ford, now known as Wallace Fard Muhammad. While specific details of his life are sketchy, Fard believed himself to be the Mahdi, the greatly anticipated Islamic messiah. Fard's mission was to educate African-Americans about the nature of their oppression by white people. Fard disappeared in 1934, but he appointed as his successor a messenger named Elijah Poole, later known as Elijah Muhammad, who led the Nation of Islam for the next forty years. Elijah Muhammad promoted the idea that Fard was God on Earth, the final prophet who was also a manifestation of Allah. This deviates significantly from traditional Islam in which the prophets are believed to be fully human, and in which Muhammad is declared to be the "seal of the prophets," meaning that no more prophets will come later.

In his book *Yakub: The Father of Mankind*, Elijah Muhammad wrote that black people were the Original People, and that they had lived in peace until the coming of white people. He went on to write that white people were created 6,000 years ago by a process called "grafting," which made them weak and their bones brittle. These white people were inferior to the Original People in every way, but were able to trick the black people and eventually enslave and oppress them, a condition that persisted until the present. Elijah Muhammad believed that in the future, this inequality will be corrected, but until then, the plight of African-Americans cannot be solved by integration. Instead, the solution is black separation from the dominant white culture and religion along with the creation of an entirely distinct state or territory. In addition, the Nation of Islam prohibits intermarriage between black and white people. Both separatism and endogamy are not widely accepted among orthodox Muslims.

Malcolm Little, more widely known as Malcolm X, was one of the many people who heard Elijah Muhammad's teachings and converted to the Nation of Islam in the 1950s. Along with Muhammad Ali, X was one of the most famous converts during this period. After discovering NOI beliefs while in prison, Malcolm X became the leader of one of the most important temples in New York; over the next decade, he drew many new followers with his fiery preaching and separatist rhetoric.

He eventually renounced Elijah Muhammad, joining instead the more traditional Sunni sect of Islam. A short time later, he was assassinated by Nation of Islam members.

The current leader, Louis Farrakhan, reformed the Nation of Islam a few years after the death of Elijah Muhammad (1897–1975). Muhammad's son, Warith Deen Mohammed, had been appointed to lead the organization at the time of his father's death. He renamed the organization World Community of al-Islam in the West, and attempted to align the teachings of the group with traditional Sunni beliefs. In response to these changes, Farrakhan, who had been a close ally of Elijah Muhammad since the 1950s, left the organization and founded a new group bearing the name Nation of Islam. Since that time, Farrakhan has been the primary leader and spokesperson of the organization.

Farrakhan's leadership in the reformed NOI has been marked by controversy, especially in relation to other minority communities. The Anti-Defamation League (CEL), a watchdog organization against anti-Semitism, has charged Farrakhan with "disseminating [a] message of hate" for routinely demonizing Jewish people and blaming them for the historic plight of African-Americans, especially in relation to economic conditions in the United States. The CEL maintains a list of some of Farrakhan's inflammatory statements. He has also commented on multiple occasions that the Jewish people cannot legitimately claim Israel as their homeland, but instead are "usurpers [and] land grabbers." Another civil rights organization, the Southern Poverty Law Center, has described Farrakhan as anti-Semitic and homophobic. The majority of the world's orthodox Muslims do not consider Farrakhan's discriminatory attitude to be acceptable.

In spite of this controversy, Farrakhan has enjoyed several well-publicized successes during his tenure. The most well known was the 1995 Million Man March, in which he encouraged African-American men to improve themselves and to work on their family relationships in an effort to overcome historic bias and oppression. The actual size of the crowd is unknown, but estimates vary between 400,000 and nearly 2 million (the higher number comes from the NOI website). Even opponents agree that the march was a successful, peaceful, and well-organized event. Farrakhan also successfully organized the Million Family March on Washington in 2000 and the reopening of a Chicago flagship mosque as an educational center in 2008.

Farrakhan's outspoken religious, political, and racial views have made him a controversial but seemingly immovable figurehead until recent years. Repeated bouts of prostate cancer, as well as extensive abdominal surgeries, have led to worries among adherents that his time is short. The identity of his future successor is unclear, as is the future of this sect whose membership has been shrinking since the 1960s.

FOR FURTHER READING

Anti-Defamation League. "Farrakhan in His Own Words." http://www.adl.org/special_reports/farrakhan_own_words2/farrakhan_own_words.asp.

Marsh, Clifton. *The Lost-Found Nation of Islam in America*. Lanham, MD: Scarecrow Press, 2000.

Muhammad, Elijah. *History of the Nation of Islam*. Phoenix: Secretarius MEMPS Publications, 1996.

Nation of Islam. "Bio Sketch of the Honorable Louis Farrakhan." http://www.noi.org/about_the_honorable_louis_farrakhan.shtml.

Southern Poverty Law Center. "Louis Farrakhan." http://www.splcenter.org/get-informed/intelligence-files/profiles/louis-farrakhan.

JEHOVAH'S WITNESSES

INTRODUCTION

Jehovah's Witnesses draw their name from the Hebrew name of God YHWH, which many people pronounce "Jehovah." The members believe that their purpose is to be witnesses of God's kingdom here on earth. Their main objective is to share the truth of the kingdom with as many people as possible before the end of time.

HISTORY

Jehovah's Witnesses grew out of Christian Protestantism, but members do not consider themselves to be Protestants. Charles Taze Russell, the founder of the Jehovah's Witness movement, had ideas which differed from traditional Christian doctrines, and he shared these ideas with a small independent Bible study group. For several years, the group met and shared Russell's beliefs with others in the same way that Witnesses do today, going from door to door. In 1879, the first issue of the *Watchtower* was published with Russell as the editor-in-chief. This group was originally called Bible Students because Russell believed every person should read the Scriptures and interpret them. Russell continued to write about his beliefs, including God's kingdom on earth, which he believed would develop soon.

After Russell's death in 1916, there was controversy surrounding who would become the next head of church. In spite of this conflict, Joseph Franklin Rutherford was elected the next president. He officially changed the name of the church to Jehovah's Witnesses in 1931. Following the death of Rutherford in 1942, Nathan Knorr became the next president. Knorr officially commissioned the New World Translation of the Bible, which is the translation used by all Jehovah's Witnesses today. Instead of referring to the text as the Old and New Testaments, Jehovah's Witnesses refer to them as the Hebrew and Greek scriptures. Some critics claim that the New World Translation is intentionally skewed to support Jehovah's Witnesses' unique beliefs and practices.

Since 1970, the church has been run not by a single president, but rather by committee. A group of ten men rotate service in the committee called the Governing Body. No women may serve on the committee.

BELIEFS

Jehovah's Witnesses are best known for their focus on evangelism. Millions of Witnesses travel door to door sharing literature and spreading their understanding of the world. Jehovah's Witnesses believe that the end of time is near, and soon God will reclaim the world to establish God's kingdom. They believe that God is the sole creator of the world, but currently the world is under the direct rule of Satan. Witnesses do not believe that a physical Jesus Christ will return, but instead that the spirit of Jesus will return. Once the world becomes God's kingdom after Christ's return, life will then become ideal.

One difference between Jehovah's Witnesses and most other Christians is that Jehovah's Witnesses reject the trinity. Jehovah's Witnesses believe that Jesus was the submissive, human son of God, not a divine incarnation. Jesus was used as a sacrifice for humankind but was assassinated on a stake rather than a cross. Because Jehovah's Witnesses do not believe that Jesus was divine, this means that God did not die for the sins of humanity. In addition, Witnesses believe that the immortality of the human soul is not unconditional, but rather resurrection of the human soul is conditional upon accepting God's gift of Jesus for humanity. Then at the end of time, all souls will be resurrected. Those who accept God will have their souls returned to their physical bodies to live in paradise here on earth. Those who do not accept Jesus will cease to exist because Jehovah's Witnesses do not believe in hell; instead, they believe that those people will have simply no afterlife at all. Additionally, only 144,000 will be accepted into heaven to help God rule this earthly paradise. Most Witnesses hope to remain on earth.

Witnesses reject all celebrations including Christmas, Easter, and birthdays because of their historical connections with paganism. They also reject traditional Christian baptism by sprinkling of water. Instead, baptism is always performed by full immersion, and it symbolizes the dedication of a person to the faith. Baptism does not remove any previous sin or provide spiritual cleansing. Additionally, there is no ordained clergy among Jehovah's Witnesses; instead, there are designated elders within each congregation who take on leadership roles. Witnesses also abstain from serving in the military, pledging allegiance to the flag, and receiving blood transfusions, stating that there are direct biblical scriptures forbidding these practices. Witnesses believe that no allegiance should be promised to any country; rather, this allegiance should only be reserved for the kingdom of God.

Worship takes place during weekly meetings in Kingdom Halls. There is no tithing among Jehovah's Witnesses. All donations are given voluntarily and often anonymously.

DEMOGRAPHICS

There are about seven million Jehovah's Witnesses worldwide, and this number is rapidly growing. In the United States, seven percent of the population identify themselves as Jehovah's Witness, which is the largest of any country. Of those who are raised in the tradition, only thirty-seven percent remain Jehovah's Witnesses into adulthood.

HARE KRISHNA

INTRODUCTION

The International Society of Krishna Consciousness (ISKCON) began in the United States in 1966. Most know the movement by the name Hare Krishna. The primary sacred text of ISKCON is the Bhagavad Gita, which centers around the deity Krishna. The Hare Krishna movement is derived from a specialized branch of Hinduism, so there are many shared concepts between ISKCON and traditional Hinduism (see the chapter on Hinduism for an overview).

HISTORY

Abhay Charan De was born in Calcutta, India, where he graduated from college, started a family, and owned a small business in the early part of his life. Then in 1950, he chose to leave his family behind and became a renunciant, dedicating himself to writing scriptural commentary. In 1966, now going by the name Abhay Charanaravinda Bhaktivedanta Swami Prabhupada, he traveled to New York City as a missionary. Wishing to spread traditional Indian beliefs to what he perceived as a spiritually bankrupt Western world, Prabhupada found a receptive audience among disenfranchised hippies, who were searching for truth in unconventional ways. Within this context, Prabhupada founded the International Society of Krishna Consciousness.

BELIEFS

Though some beliefs are similar to Hinduism, there
are also many differences. Hare Krishnas primarily
worship Krishna, and they see him as being the "supreme
godhead," the greatest deity from whom all else emanates.
For this reason, Hare Krishnas describe themselves as
monotheistic. The name Hare Krishna comes from the
common chant: "Hare Krishna, Hare Krishna, Krishna
Krishna, Hare Hare." Hare literally means "praise," and
Hare Krishnas believe that the act of chanting Krishna's
name actually calls him into physical presence among the
chanters. Therefore, the frequent chanting of Krishna's
name invites him into the world to bless all who hear.
Hare Krishnas also may chant the name of Radha,
Krishna's wife. Honoring Krishnas' female counterpart is
an affirmation of the interdependence of male and female.
Hare Krishnas openly reject social inequalities based on
caste, class, and gender.

Perhaps one of the biggest differences between Hindus
and Hare Krishnas is their stance on evangelism. For most
Hindus, religion is a part of life and culture from birth;
Hinduism is something one is born into, not something
one chooses. As a result, there is no such thing as
conversion to Hinduism, and most Hindus are not seeking
new believers. Hare Krishnas, on the other hand, believe
strongly in sharing and spreading the spiritual truths of
Krishna. Many people are familiar with the presence of
Hare Krishnas in public places, passing out literature to
passers-by and spreading their beliefs. Hare Krishnas are
also known for their charity, frequently opening their

temple doors and providing free meals to the community
as a means of spreading their faith.

As with many Hindus, most Hare Krishnas are
vegetarian. Hare Krishnas believe in submission to
dharma (moral and religious obligation), which includes
avoiding intoxicants, refusing inappropriate sexual
relationships, and practicing nonviolence. Many Hare
Krishna men shave their heads, leaving only a single
lock of hair on the back of the head; head shaving is a
traditional Indian sign of renunciation, so this practice
also is part of Buddhism and other forms of Hinduism.
However, only Hare Krishnas leave the lock of hair on the
head, demonstrating the commitment they have made to
Krishna.

DEMOGRAPHICS

Though headquartered in San Francisco, California,
there are Hare Krishnas all over the world. According
to ISKCON's official register, there are approximately
250,000 members worldwide. The International Society
of Krishna Consciousness movement enjoyed its greatest
popularity when Prabhupada was still alive (1966–77);
however, it still continues to gain new converts. In
recent years, ISKCON has attracted a growing number
of Indian devotees, most of whom convert from
traditional Hinduism. Many of these converts view
ISKCON's rejection of caste differences, promotion of
gender equality, and monotheistic beliefs as being more
compatible with the modern world.

UNIQUELY AMERICAN TRADITIONS COMPARED TO CHRISTIANITY

	NATURE OF GOD	NATURE OF HUMANITY	NATURE OF THE UNIVERSE	NATURE OF RELIGION	FOUNDERS AND TEXTS
CHRISTIANITY	One creator-God in three persons: Father, Son, and Holy Spirit. God is personal interacts with humanity, is all-knowing, and all-powerful.	God allows humans free will to choose between right and wrong. However, they are inherently sinful and are incapable of achieving salvation on their own. Ultimately, salvation only comes through God.	This world is temporary. We are engaged in a battle between good and evil. Someday God will judge all people at the end of time, which will bring the long-awaited coming of the "Kingdom of God."	Through belief in Jesus Christ, humans are saved from sin and will have eternal life after death. Because Jesus is the supreme sacrifice to atone for the sins of humanity, Christianity is the only path to salvation.	The founders were followers of Jesus of Nazareth, born sometime between 7 BCE and 1 CE. Texts include the Bible (including Old and New Testaments) and, for some Christians, the Apocrypha.
MORMONISM	The three persons of the Trinity are separate entities, with the Father and Son having material bodies and the Holy Spirit a spiritual body. Other gods exist whom Mormons do not worship alongside the Godhead.	Human souls are eternal, not created. Rejecting the notion of original sin, Mormons believe people are capable of achieving perfection and achieving godly status, which is called reaching Exaltation.	The universe is eternal, having no beginning and no end, but he only organized pre-existing matter. Mormons also expect a Last Judgment, when God will send people to one of four kingdoms, based on their actions both during and after life.	Mormons believe that the early Christian church corrupted the truth of Jesus' message, and Joseph Smith reinstated this truth. People still have the opportunity to receive and accept this message even after death.	Joseph Smith founded the Latter Day Saints movement during the 1800s, when he received the revelation of the Book of Mormon—considered to be divinely inspired alongside the Old and New Testaments.

228

	NATURE OF GOD	NATURE OF HUMANITY	NATURE OF THE UNIVERSE	NATURE OF RELIGION	FOUNDERS AND TEXTS
UNITARIAN	One unified God, not triune in nature. Though most Unitarian Universalists are monotheistic, individual perspectives on the nature of God vary from person to person within the tradition.	All humans deserve respect and should be treated accordingly, and should act with freedom and responsibility.	One guiding principle is "the respect for the interdependent web of existence, of which we all are a part." Though each person has a unique view, most UUs value living in harmony with the natural world.	Unitarians reject the idea of absolute truth and accept the validity of many religious traditions, including non-Christian traditions. Each individual engages in a unique quest for his or her own truth.	Unitarians and Universalists merged to form Unitarian Universalism in 1961. Both original movements have roots in 16th-century Europe. Sacred texts of many traditions are respected, including the Bible.
SCIENTOLOGY	Scientology affirms existence in a Supreme Being, though its nature remains largely undefined.	People store negative experiences from present and past lives (both on earth and other planets), leading to irrational behavior. Therefore, they must rationally release this baggage to find happiness.	The physical world is a product of human consciousness and has no reality apart from our experience of it. Over time, people have forgotten the true spiritual nature of the universe, mistaking the material world for reality.	Scientology provides an organized series of steps to release obstructions from individual souls, called thetans, through a process called the Bridge to Total Freedom.	Science fiction author L. Ron Hubbard founded Scientology in 1954. The most famous Scientologist text is Hubbard's Dianetics.

UNIQUELY AMERICAN TRADITIONS COMPARED *continued*

	NATURE OF GOD	NATURE OF HUMANITY	NATURE OF THE UNIVERSE	NATURE OF RELIGION	FOUNDERS AND TEXTS
ANABAPTISTS (AMISH/MENNONITE/QUAKER)	As Christian Protestants, these groups also believe in one, omniscient, omnipotent creator-God alongside the Son and the Holy Spirit	People should be responsible for their own spiritual well-being. Therefore, baptism should not be performed until a person can confess his or her own faith.	The material world distracts from spiritual focus, so interaction with it should be limited.	Human beings are highly fallible, and as such, need the repeated cleansing and renewal of baptism.	The original Anabaptist movement has roots in 16th-century Europe.
NATION OF ISLAM (NOI)	The NOI shares with other Muslims a belief in the supreme oneness of God, or Allah.	Racial differences between black and white have origins at the time of creation. Black people are the Original People and are superior, and therefore should remain separate.	Whereas Allah created black people, white people were scientifically created in a black laboratory 6,000 years ago.	In addition to following the Five Pillars of Islam, NOI adherents also subscribe to black separatism. Therefore, religion is a source of racial and political empowerment, going beyond the spiritual realm alone.	The NOI was founded in 1930 by Wallace Fard Muhammad, who is believed to be the Mahdi—a messianic figure in Islam. The Qur'an is the most sacred text.

	NATURE OF GOD	NATURE OF HUMANITY	NATURE OF THE UNIVERSE	NATURE OF RELIGION	FOUNDERS AND TEXTS
JEHOVAH'S WITNESSES	One true creator-God, called Jehovah. Witnesses reject the Trinity and instead consider Jehovah to be a single, unified deity.	Human beings should aim to obey and glorify Jehovah in all things. Through evangelism and moral living, people may strive to earn a place in God's kingdom. Only 144,000 people will go to Heaven; the rest of the righteous will live in earthly paradise at the end times.	Though Jehovah created the universe, the world is under Satan's rule. One day all humanity will be resurrected, judged, and retested over another 1,000 years. Afterward, Jehovah will rule over a newly restored paradise on earth.	Unlike mainstream Christians, Witnesses reject the divinity of Jesus. They see Jesus as God's first creation. The goal of religion is to show people the way to final, eternal paradise—not in the afterlife, but in the present world after Armageddon.	Charles Taze Russell founded the Jehovah's Witness movement in the 1870s. While the Christian Bible is their sacred text, Jehovah's Witnesses have their own unique translation called the New World Translation.
HARE KRISHNA (ISKCON)	The Hindu god Krishna is the "Supreme Godhead" in ISKCON. Krishna relates to his devotees through familiar loving relationships: parent-child, husband-wife, friend-friend.	Humans are spiritual beings who temporarily occupy physical bodies through repeated lifetimes. People must work to overcome material obstacles so that they may be spiritually united with Krishna.	Krishna created the universe and all living beings out of his own divine essence. Therefore, all things are a reflection of Krishna, though an imperfect one.	Through devotion to Krishna, which includes service and mediation, people may achieve spiritual freedom. The cycle of reincarnation will end, and the devotee will finally be reunited with Krishna to live with him for all eternity.	Prabhupada brought his message from India to the United States in 1965. The Bhagavad Gita and the Bhagavata Purana are the most revered texts in ISKCON, though there are also many more supplemental texts.

POP CULTURE-BASED RELIGIONS AND BELIEFS

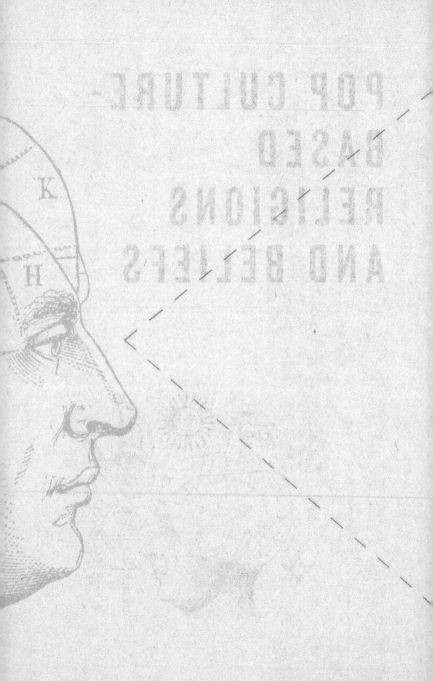

Vampirism

INTRODUCTION

Vampirism is a new religious movement of personal empowerment whose practitioners seek to increase their spiritual, cosmic power by "feeding" off the life force of other people or animals. Some vampires (also called vampyres) believe that this energy is uniquely present in blood or other fluid exchanges, and are generally known as sanguinarian or pranic vampires. Others believe this life force can also be consumed through various types of strong emotional exchanges such as love, seduction, or intimidation; these are most commonly called psychic vampires.

HISTORY

As with other new religions, Vampirism is often spread via the internet, chat rooms, Facebook groups, and web sites. These central organizers of Vampirism are independent and locally controlled, making Vampirism even more difficult to categorically define. Many vampire web sites use black backgrounds and Goth artwork, and have graphics of dripping blood. Additionally, like the sites themselves, many who participate in the vampire subculture do embrace cultural stereotypes by getting fangs or dressing in corsets, capes, or all black.

However, in spite of these stereotypical appearances, web sites promoting the vampire subculture are vehement that "real" vampires do not resemble the creatures of television, books, and movies. According to www.drinkdeeplyanddream.com, vampires are the people next door, not nocturnal killers. Vampire groups generally claim that they are not violent or evil, and many local groups, often called covens, have established moral codes for the exchange of blood or psychic energy that do not cause harm (see Rose). Among the few cases in which criminals have claimed to be vampires, they appear to use vampirism as an excuse for illegal behavior (see Glynn).

BELIEFS

Belief systems of the vampire subculture are diverse, and no religious hierarchy establishes dogma or practice for all believers. It is difficult to generalize about vampire beliefs, worldview, morality, or philosophy because some practitioners may also claim to be part of other traditions like Christianity, Neopaganism, ancient religions (such as Greco-Roman, Egyptian, or Sumerian), Occultism, Wicca, or Islam. Syncretism, the combining of different religious traditions, is common, and many vampires are explicitly syncretic in describing their traditions and practices.

The Vampire Church exemplifies vampires' pluralist and nonhierarchical approach to religion (www.vampire -church.com). This organization claims to have nearly 1,700 members and does not claim affiliation with any religious group. However, they do employ religious terms. For example, the object of the vampire's feeding is called *chi*, a description of supernatural life force in Chinese traditional religion. One contributor to the Vampire Church web site refers to humans having an "aura," a concept drawn from New Age religions. Other subjects on the website include magick, from Neopaganism, and the Nephilim, which has roots in Judaism. Additionally, in the name of the group itself, the Christian concept of a church as a gathering of believers is employed. However, in spite of these religious elements, the author still claims repeatedly that Vampirism is not a religion at all.

The Vampire Temple, another Vampirist website, is more explicitly religious but still draws from diverse religious traditions (www.vampiretemple.com). For example, the Vampire Creed denies the monotheistic idea of God in the Abrahamic religions, but also claims, "I [the individual] am the only God there is." Another seeming contradiction is the Vampire Temple's professed belief in rationalism as well as the reality of magic. Vampires using this website can implement the basic teachings of the creed via *The Vampire Bible* and its interpretations, called revelations, by becoming a ritual practitioner known as a Nightside Vampire.

DEMOGRAPHICS

Vampires have a few key rituals or beliefs in common; they are also diverse, local, independent, and prone to change. However, this does not mean that these "real" vampire communities are not religious, but rather that they are very different types of religion than we might initially recognize. As such, it is difficult to know exactly how many people claim Vampirism as their religion.

FOR FURTHER READING

Glynn, Casey. "Fla. Murder Suspect Claims She's Part Vampire, Part Werewolf." http://www.cbsnews.com/8301-504083_162-20112703 -504083.html (September 28, 2011).

Crewdson, Michael and Margaret Mittlebach. "To Die For: Painting the Town Red, and the Capes and Nails Black." *New York Times* (November 24, 2000).

Rose, Lisa. "N.J. Vampire Subculture Thrives on Blood, Rituals, Fangs." *The New Jersey Star-Ledger* (October 15, 2009).

JEDIISM

INTRODUCTION

Jediism is a recent religious movement aligned with
the Jedi principles professed in the *Star Wars* movies.
Referring to themselves as Jedi apprentices, knights,
and masters, practitioners believe that an omnipresent,
impersonal Force governs the universe. Jedis are able
to connect with one another via websites and internet
discussion, though they also gather for conventions to
connect with other Jedis. In some limited areas, if there
are enough practitioners in close proximity to one another,
Jedis are able to form physical communities and conduct
rituals unique to each individual group as well.

HISTORY

While Jedis generally avoid hierarchy and value autonomy,
several major independent centers of Jedi religion have
sprouted recently. In Texas, the Temple of the Jedi
Order was founded in 2005 by John Henry Phelan,
called Brother John, and has been at the forefront of
organizing and articulating Jedi beliefs in the United
States. In conjunction with the internet organization
religioustolerance.org, Jedis from this temple developed
a set of key moral principles for their community, as well
as conditions for membership and advancement. In New
Zealand, the Jedi Church has developed and publicized
a similar belief statement, though their standards for
participation are minimal in comparison to the Temple of

the Jedi Order. The Jedi Church web site reads, "It's easy to join the Jedi church; just look inside yourself, and feel the force." These two Jedi organizations and others like them use internet message boards to conduct worship and education, and also to connect practitioners with one another. They have also used the internet to organize massive census campaigns over the past ten years.

BELIEFS

The principles of Jedi Code are by design syncretistic, meaning they combine the beliefs and ideas of many known religions. Jedis are quick to claim that while their religious beliefs mirror the principles of the *Star Wars* movies, they are not simply role playing the movies; instead, practitioners are committed to living day-to-day "in touch with the Living Force flowing through and around" them (http://www.templeofthejediorder.org/home/doctrine). Jedis further believe that the power of the Force has been present in the lives of real historical figures, to whom they refer as Jedi masters, including Lao Tzu, Jesus, the Buddha, St. Francis of Assisi, and Gandhi, who shared a common commitment to peace and illumination (see www.templeofthejediorder.org/home/doctrine). A Jedi attempts to learn from these various masters and seeks to live according to the principles of the Jedi Code (http://www.jediism.org/generic0.html), which is a combination of the beliefs of many established religions like Taoism, Christianity, Buddhism, and Shinto.

DEMOGRAPHICS

Jedi religion was the source of some controversy during recent national censuses in England and New Zealand. In each of these countries, a campaign was conducted via the internet to encourage citizens to list their religion as "Jedi" or "Jedi Knight." In England during the 2001 census, 390,000 residents listed Jediism as their religion. Likewise in New Zealand, Jediism was listed as the religion of choice by 53,000 people in the 2001 census, and a campaign is currently underway for the 2011 census as well. Advocates at the Jedi Church in New Zealand are promoting their efforts as a protest in favor of religious liberty, noting, "Remember that in a free country . . . you have the freedom to decide what your religion is, and no one has the right to take away that civil liberty by categorizing your religion as anything other than the legible answer you provide them" (http://www.jedichurch .org/census2011). Part of what makes Jediism and religious movements like it so intriguing is the concerted effort to use the internet to spread the group's ideals.

FOR FURTHER READING

http://www.jediism.org/

Office of National Statistics. "390,000 Jedi There Are." http://www .ons.gov.uk/ons/rel/census/census-2001-summary-theme-figures-and -rankings/390-000-jedis-there-are/jedi.html.

Perrott, Alan. "Jedi Order Lures 53,000 Disciples." *New Zealand Herald* (Aug. 31, 2002).

Temple of the Jedi Order. http://www.templeofthejediorder.org/.

DIVINING, ASTROLOGY, TAROT CARDS AND NEW AGE

INTRODUCTION

Divination, astrology, and the use of tarot cards all stem from a common belief in the ability to predict the future, or fortune telling. These and similar practices have existed since ancient times, but today they are most often associated with the religious movement known as New Age.

HISTORY

The New Age movement likely developed out of the nineteenth century Theosophy movement, which refers to the pursuit of divine wisdom through the union of the physical and metaphysical worlds. New Age thought was further influenced by twentieth century psychology and the West's rediscovery of Eastern religion and philosophy. Eventually, New Age went mainstream in the 1970s with the endorsement of celebrities like Shirley MacLaine, and then the movement continued to prosper, thanks to the later success of health gurus like Andrew Weil and Deepak Chopra. However, the movement has also come under sharp criticism from members of the scientific community and other skeptics who believe that astrology, crystal healing, and other forms of New Age spirituality are pseudoscience with no evidence of success.

BELIEFS

The New Age movement takes cues from many world religions, thereby creating a belief system that is less rigid than most. New Age spirituality contains aspects of monotheistic, polytheistic, and nontheistic traditions, including Islam, Buddhism, Taoism, and Neopaganism, while also channeling psychology, physics, and natural healing. New Age practitioners believe strongly in the interconnectedness of mind, body, and spirit, and promote the belief that human beings are on the verge of a massive cultural shift toward total understanding and peace. The name "New Age" comes from the belief that there is the potential within each person to bring this new age—this shift—into being by drawing upon cosmic energies and forces. Therefore, New Age practitioners engage in a wide variety of self-actualization practices, including meditation, holistic healing, and divination practices like tarot card reading and astrology.

Divination is the attempt to determine the future, often through communication with supernatural forces. New Agers believe that divination is a way of accessing cosmic knowledge for our own betterment and self-realization, thereby moving us closer to the new age. Two common forms of divination are astrology (discerning the future by the stars and planets) and cartomancy (using cards to discern one's fate). Astrological divination is commonly associated with the horoscope, which is based on the position of the stars and planets at the time of one's birth. In addition, the use of a tarot deck, a series of

78 cards with pictures that represent aspects of a person's life or future choices, is an example of cartomancy.

DEMOGRAPHICS

Recent surveys in the United States indicate that people who identify their religion as New Age make up a tiny minority of the population (less than a half percent), but that many more believe in the ideals or have tried the practices of this movement. For example, in the United States, twenty-eight percent of respondents to a Gallup poll in 2000 stated that they believed in astrology (see Wynn).

FOR FURTHER READING

Gardner, Michael. *The New Age: Notes of a Fringe Watcher.* New York: Prometheus Books, 1990.

MacLaine, Shirley. *Out on a Limb.* New York: Bantam, 1983.

Shermer, Michael, ed. *The Skeptic's Guide to Pseudoscience.* Santa Barbara: ABC-CLIO, Inc., 2002.

Wynn, Charles. "Seen Any Red Pandas Lately?" *Journal of College Science Teaching* 36.5 (2007): 10–11.

BELIEF IN
THE PARANORMAL
AND SPIRITS

INTRODUCTION

Central to paranormal and spiritual beliefs is an idea
that some aspect of the person—often a spirit or soul—
survives death and continues to be present in some way in
the material world. In this belief system, the spirits of the
deceased are often connected to a certain place or object,
and these spirits are still able to communicate with the
living.

Belief in the paranormal has gained popularity in
recent years. Fascination with the spiritual realm is
present in numerous popular television shows related
to ghosts and hauntings, including *Ghost Hunters* on the
SyFy network and *Paranormal State* on A&E, in which
teams investigate alleged hauntings. Skeptics contend that
shows like these manipulate viewers by means of camera
tricks and pseudoscientific language, and that paranormal
beliefs are unsubstantiated by actual scientific inquiry.

HISTORY AND BELIEFS

Belief in spirits, ghosts, and people's ability to contact
them is not a new phenomenon. Scholars have identified
animism, or the conviction that everything has a spirit,
as one of the earliest religious beliefs of humans. Ghosts
figure prominently in the religious beliefs of many ancient

cultures, including Egyptian, Greco-Roman, Chinese, Japanese, and Tibetan cultures; efforts were made in these cultures to communicate with and to appease the spirits of those who had died but not entirely departed. In the Bible, King Saul goes to a medium to try to contact Samuel (1 Sam. 28), and there are laws forbidding such practices in the Old Testament, indicating that belief in the paranormal existed in ancient Israel. In Europe and the United States, the Spiritualist Church is a movement in which people attempt to contact the dead through séances, the interpretation of knocking sounds, mediumship, and other means. Though Spiritualism reached its height of popularity in the late nineteenth and early twentieth centuries, it continues to be practiced today.

DEMOGRAPHICS

In a 2005 Gallup Poll, three in four Americans expressed a belief in some form of paranormal activity, including extrasensory perception, clairvoyance and other forms of mind control or communication, ghosts and haunted houses, and channeling, which is the inhabitation of a living person by a spirit. In this same survey, more than one third of respondents agreed that "houses can be haunted," and nearly the same number concurred that "the spirits of dead people can come back in certain places." In a poll conducted by CBS News in 2009, forty-eight percent of Americans stated a belief in ghosts, and more than one in five Americans claimed to have seen a ghost.

FOR FURTHER READING

Alfano, Sean. "Poll: Majority Believe In Ghosts." CBS News. http://www.cbsnews.com/stories/2005/10/29/opinion/polls/main994766.shtml.

Moore, David W. "Three in Four Americans Believe in Paranormal." Gallup. http://www.gallup.com/poll/16915/three-four-americans-believe-paranormal.aspx.

Shermer, Michael. *Why People Believe in Weird Things: Pseudoscience, Superstition, and Confusions of Our Time*. New York: Henry Holt, 2002.

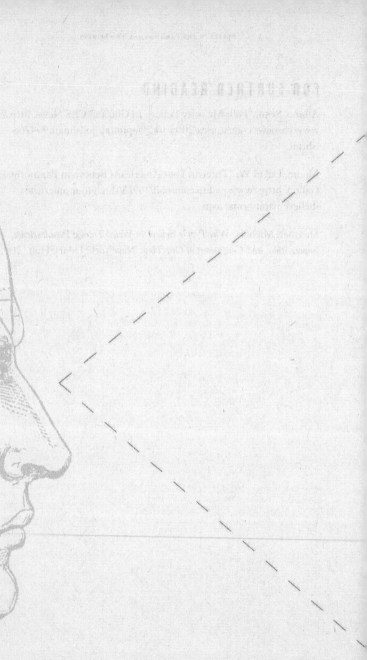

DEMONOLOGY AND ANGELOLOGY

Many religious traditions share a belief in the presence
of spiritual beings who influence earthly human affairs.
Some of these beings are forces for good, representing
order, and some are forces for evil or disorder, and they
often possess humanlike qualities or sentience. These
divine beings are commonly described as angels and
demons, although names vary widely among different
traditions. Popular beliefs involving angels and demons
are often an attempt to answer the question of why bad
things happen in the world.

WESTERN RELIGIONS

Judaism

Angelic beings including cherubim and seraphim
populate much of ancient Jewish scripture. However, these
beings bear little resemblance to the kindly guardian
angels of popular belief. Some biblical angels are fierce;
for example, they have flaming swords (Gen. 3:24) and
lead armies into battle (Ex. 23:23). Others are messengers,
bringing news of impending destruction (Gen. 19:15).
Still others seem more like lawyers; in Job, they are
members of a "court," including a prosecuting attorney. In
Hebrew, the name for the prosecuting angel is ha-Satan,
or "the Accuser"; though this figure may be a precursor
to the Satan who later appears in the New Testament, in
this context the Accuser is just another member of the

heavenly court, not a diabolical force. The cherubim and seraphim have multiple sets of wings and can fly (Isa. 6:2, Ezek. 10:3). The closest an angel comes to being a personal guide to humans in the Hebrew Bible occurs when Gabriel becomes an interpreter in Daniel 8.

While angelic beings are common, very little is mentioned in the Hebrew Bible about demons. Though the King James Version includes the translation of several words as "demon" in the Hebrew Bible, a better translation for these words would be "idols" because they are actually objects of worship, not beings with spiritual powers (see Ps. 106:37). Discussion of spirits do occur in some places in the Hebrew Bible. For example, the "spirit of jealousy" afflicts people in Numbers 5:14, and a "bad spirit" torments Saul in 1 Samuel 16:14. However, these are not evil forces opposed to God, especially since in the second case it is God who actually sends the spirit. Instead, it seems that "spirits" here refer to chaotic human dispositions, rather than to real spiritual beings.

Christianity

As in the Hebrew Bible, in the Christian New Testament angels are not simply gentle guides. The angel who visits Mary tells her, "Do not be afraid," indicating that fear is her natural response to this encounter, and a similar admonition is given by the heavenly armies who meet the shepherds in Luke 1:30 and 2:10. The angels of Revelation are exceedingly fierce; they transform water into blood and release thunder and earthquakes, destroying a third of the earth, including humans (Rev. 8). In the same text, the angel Michael fights a war against a dragon, which results in the expulsion of other angels from heaven at the end of time (Revelation 12).

Because their writers were influenced by Greek and Roman ideas of beings called daimons, early Christian texts are more populated with malevolent spirits than is the Hebrew Bible. Jesus often casts out demons, including those who cause mental illness and physical disability (Mark 5:1–20; 9:14–28). The evil being called Satan in Mark and a devil in Matthew and Luke is responsible for the temptation of Jesus before his public ministry. In the epistles, demons are understood as forces who might cause believers to renounce their faith, and in Revelation, demons lead an army at Armageddon.

Islam

In the Qur'an, there are references to many angels who also appear in the Christian Bible. For example, both Jibril (Gabriel in Christian texts) and Mikhail (Michael) appear in surah 2, where they are portrayed alongside Allah as second in command against the unbelievers (2:97–98). Jibril is the most prominent among the angels, since he is responsible for delivering the revelation of the Qur'an to Muhammad. As in the Jewish and Christian scriptures, Islamic angels are messengers (22:75; 35:1), militaristic (8:9–12), and guard-like (13:11). Generally, angels are totally obedient to Allah. For Muslims, the belief in angels is one of the Six Articles of Faith.

In the Qur'an, there are also spirits called jinn, whose origin in Arabian culture long predates Islam. Unlike angels, who are subservient to Allah, jinn can exhibit a wide range of natures and allegiances; sometimes they are helpful spirits, and at other times they are disruptive. They are also occasionally "audacious" (27:39) and transgressive (18:50). According to the Qur'an, Allah created the jinn out of fire, with their initial purpose being to serve Allah (15:27; 51:56). Much more malevolent, however, are the shaitans, the foremost of whom is named Iblis. The shaitans are spirits who are responsible for the fall of humanity and who taught them sorcery (2:36, 102). The shaitans, particularly Iblis, are the true enemies of both Allah and humanity, and they are most responsible for leading believers astray (2:178, 208). The word *shaitan* comes from the same origin as the word *Satan* in Christianity.

ASIAN AND INDIGENOUS RELIGIONS

South Asian religious cosmologies also feature spiritual beings, although their opposition to one another is differently focused than in Western traditions. In Hinduism, for example, the gods (devas) and demons (asuras) are constantly locked in battle, but not necessarily because one is good and the other evil. Rather, the primary difference between the devas and asuras is that the devas ultimately submit to their dharma, or religious duty. In contrast, the asuras are self-absorbed and submit neither to the gods nor to dharma. Without this submission, the world is in danger of spinning into chaos; therefore, the opposition between the devas and asuras is not one between good and evil, but rather between submission and selfishness, and ultimately between order and disorder.

Buddhists also have sacred stories that involve demons; one of the most famous is the story of Siddhartha's meditation under the Bodhi tree, the tree of enlightenment, when he is assailed by the demon Mara, the lord of death, as a final temptation before achieving enlightenment. As in Hinduism, in Buddhism demons are a force of chaos or disorder instead of moral evil. For example, demons sometimes interfere with the practices of holy people trying to improve their karma, as well as creating restlessness in regular humans. Some demons are actually ghosts, the spirits of the dead who bother the living for food and drink.

Demons and evil spirits also play a role in East Asian religions. For example, in Japanese lore, spirits called Oni are commonly associated with natural evil, such as strong winds, bad harvest, or miscarriage more than moral evil. Traditional Chinese religion incorporates rituals to both thwart and appease restless ghosts, demons, and other evil spirits. In both Chinese and Japanese religion, evil spirits are forces which can disrupt people's lives and bring hardship or disaster if they are unhappy. Again, these spirits represent chaos, whereas religious ritual is used as a tool to restore order.

Additionally, many indigenous religions incorporate a belief in spiritual beings. The general term for this belief in a spiritual realm is animism, which extends beyond a simple understanding of angels and demons and includes a vast number of spirits that populate the world. In Zimbabwean indigenous religion, Shavi produce both illness and healing. In many Native American beliefs, human shamans are guided by nature-spirits and can be possessed by them. In New Zealand, the Maori mythology is populated with spirits of light, darkness, cosmos, and chaos. Once more, the spirit world serves as an arena in which guardians of both chaos and order can interact with the human world.

POPULAR BELIEFS

In both Judaism and Christianity, beliefs in angels and demons became more prominent after the closing of each canon. In Judaism, post-biblical literature moves far beyond the Hebrew Bible when it comes to describing the nature and function of demons in the world. For example, in the Talmud and rabbinic midrash, we learn of the demon Lilith, who is associated with death in sleep and harm to newborns unless proper amulets are used to repel her. In the book of Enoch, which was written under an assumed name, we get descriptions of fallen angels who choose to pursue human women, which causes them to be ejected from heaven for all time. Kabbalist mysticism posits an entire hierarchy of angels and demons who inhabit sephirot, ladders or paths to the divine. Post-biblical Christian tradition similarly expands the roles of angels and demons, perhaps best exemplified by the writings of Dante, who populates heaven, hell, and purgatory with all manner of divine beings in his *Divine Comedy*. Dante's writings also likely influenced the Christian concept of Satan's fall from God, an idea not found in biblical literature.

According to key findings in the Religious Landscape Survey conducted by the Pew Forum, sixty-eight percent of Americans believe that angels and demons are active in the world. Belief in angels has been profoundly important in the New Age movement, which has flourished in the United States since the 1970s. Many New Age beliefs draw on Christian and Jewish concepts of an angelic hierarchy, terminology such as cherubim and seraphim, and the belief that angels are involved in spiritual battles on earth. However, New Age angels tend not to be as fierce as their biblical counterparts but are instead described as guides, teachers, or contacts with the spirit realm. Some New Age philosophers also describe these non-human beings as nature-forces, elementals, or spirit guides. Many New Age practitioners believe that these spirits can be channeled through a medium, who acts as the angel's mouthpiece to communicate guidance to the seeker. The widespread appeal of such a belief system has been evident in the massive sales of such works as James Redfield's *Celestine Prophecy* and Sylvia Browne's *Book of Angels*.

Demonology and angelology figure prominently in conservative Christian beliefs as well, as popularized by the fiction of Frank Peretti and the apologetic work by Billy Graham titled *Angels*. These authors tend to stress the biblical roles of angels, including those of guard and warrior, while at the same time strengthening their connection to the world and emphasizing their participation in day-to-day human affairs. In Catholic Christian traditions, demons are still believed to interfere in human life, as indicated by the continued presence of exorcism training courses for clergy and bishops. For example, the Catholic News Agency recently reported on an exorcism training event in Baltimore, Maryland

(http://www.catholicnewsagency.com/news/over-100
-catholic-clergy-attend-exorcism-training-in-baltimore).

What accounts for the proliferation of popular beliefs
in angels and demons, as well as the wide-ranging ancient
beliefs behind them? There are many possible answers,
but in part, these convictions may be attempts to explain
the existence of evil and chaos in the world. In both
ancient and modern times, people have striven to answer
the existential question, "Why do bad things happen?"
The presence of invisible forces, outside of human control
but active in human affairs, offers a compelling answer for
many people.

FOR FURTHER READING

Clark, Lynn Schofield. *From Angels to Aliens: Teenagers, the Media, and the Supernatural*. Oxford: Oxford University Press, 2003.

Santana, Richard W. and Gregory Erickson. "Demons, Aliens, and Spiritual Warfare: Belief and Reality." In *Religion and Popular Culture: Rescripting the Sacred*. Richard W. Santana and Gregory Erickson, eds. Jefferson, NC: MacFarland, 2008.

Pew Forum on Religion and Public Life. "U.S. Religious Landscape Survey: Summary of Key Findings." http://religions.pewforum.org/pdf/report-religious-landscape-study-key-findings.pdf.

FANDOM

It might seem odd to encounter the topic of fandom in a book about religion. Fandom is a product of popular culture and mass media, whereas religions ought to transcend that mundane sort of experience. On closer inspection, however, there is much in common between fan culture and overt forms of religious expression. This discussion of fandom in popular culture will attempt to offer at least a cursory look at the overlap between the two.

Fandom is the blanket term for any of a number of communities that obsessively follow some element of popular culture. There are fandoms for TV shows (*Buffy the Vampire Slayer, Doctor Who, Star Trek*), books (*Harry Potter, Lord of the Rings*), movies (*The Big Lebowski, The Rocky Horror Picture Show*), music (Elvis, Justin Bieber), and sports teams. Serious fans are not just passive recipients of the mass culture they enjoy. Rather, they produce responses to the objects of their fandom, including fanzines, fan fiction, games, podcasts, and visual and performance art. Fans gather together for conventions and discussion groups, and travel specifically to see sites mentioned in the series, show, or song. Scholars who study fan culture have warned against dismissing the broad and creative realm of fandom as "kooky" or full of social misfits. Instead, they have emphasized the ways fan culture carefully examines the media, offers a source for consumer activism, creates beauty, and provides alternative communities (see Jenkins).

Both people of faith and people who are seriously engaged in fandom build community in similar ways, trying to give meaning to human experience. When sociologists talk about how religion functions, they mention the importance of shared rituals and activities that promote a feeling of unity. Psychologists discuss the ability of religious practice to ease fear and provide comfort in difficult situations. Additionally, anthropologists identify the importance of religion in the production of art, literature, and material culture. Fandoms function for their participants in much the same way as religion. For example, in *Star Trek* fandom, fans see themselves as a community not only with shared rituals (conventions, dress, language), but also with a meaningful philosophy and ethical system for living out the universal themes of the show (rationality, exploration, humanism). From this experience of unity, *Star Trek* fans produce art, literature, videos, and other forms of expression that display their allegiance not only to the show itself, but also to the values portrayed therein. Taken as a whole, the way *Star Trek* fandom functions bears a striking similarity to the way religions work in the lives of adherents. Roger Nygard's documentary *Trekkies* (1997) illustrates the religious and ethical aspects of *Star Trek* fan conventions. *Star Trek* fandom is one of the most widely studied among academics who seek parallels between fan culture and religion. Jediism in *Star Wars* fandom is another example of a fan culture with profoundly religious overtones.

Besides giving us insight into the ways communities function, understanding how fandom operates in the lives of its participants helps us to recognize the widespread influence of popular media on our society's sense of reality and culture. Historically, more established religions like Christianity had the deepest impact on most people's ideas and behaviors concerning morality and values, but for many people today mass media has supplanted the influence of churches and synagogues, to a great extent. These forms of entertainment and the communities that surround them offer a different avenue for the transmission of morality and values.

FOR FURTHER READING

Doss, Erika. *Elvis Culture: Fans, Faith & Image*. Lawrence: University of Kansas Press, 1999.

Jenkins, Henry. *Textual Poachers: Television Fans and Participatory Culture*. New York: Routledge, 1992.

Jindra, Michael. "Star Trek Fandom as a Religious Phenomenon." *Sociology of Religion* 55:1 (Spring, 1994) 27–51.

POP CULTURE-BASED RELIGIONS COMPARED TO CHRISTIANITY

	NATURE OF THE SUPERNATURAL	NATURE OF HUMANITY	NATURE OF THE UNIVERSE
CHRISTIANITY	One creator-God in three persons: Father, Son, and Holy Spirit. God is personal and interacts with humanity, is all-knowing, and all-powerful.	God allows humans free will to choose between right and wrong. However, they are inherently sinful and are incapable of achieving salvation on their own. Ultimately, salvation only comes through God.	This world is temporary. We are engaged in a battle between good and evil. Someday God will judge all people at the end of time, which will bring the long-awaited coming of the "Kingdom of God."
VAMPIRISM	No specific belief in deities or other supernatural forces is universal among practitioners.	Humans are able to feed on the "life force" of other people, either physically through fluids or psychically through energy exchange.	Diverse views of the universe are represented throughout Vampirism.
JEDIISM	The Force is an animating energy in the universe similar to the concept of qi in Chinese religion. The Force has also been compared to the Tao in Taoism.	Human beings may tap into The Force through the heightened awareness achieved through Jediism. Living by Jedi principles should prompt people to act ethically.	Previous Jedi masters—including Jesus, Gandhi, and the Buddha—reveal truths about the universe and The Force. Specifics regarding these truths vary by group and individual.
DIVINING/ASTROLOGY/TAROT/NEW AGE	Contains aspects of monotheistic, polytheistic, and nontheistic traditions. These practices all assume the presence of a spirit world in some form, though specifics may vary.	The mind, body, and spirit are interconnected. Humans are on the verge of reaching a new age of peace and understanding through practices which include meditation, holistic healing, and divination.	Human beings are able to predict the future, tapping into a spiritual plane in order to obtain supernatural guidance and heightened spiritual awareness.

	NATURE OF THE SUPERNATURAL	NATURE OF HUMANITY	NATURE OF THE UNIVERSE
PARANORMAL/SPIRITS	A belief in the spirit world, which includes the enduring nature of souls, underscores the belief in the paranormal.	Human souls or spirits remain on earth after death, and they are able to communicate with those who are still living, often through a medium.	Places and objects throughout the material world are filled with spiritual significance. These entities may serve as conduits through which living people and spirits may communicate and interact.
DEMONOLOGY/ANGELOLOGY	Demons and angels—or more generally, evil or good spirits—inhabit the universe and have an impact on earthly affairs.	These good and evil spirits possess humanlike qualities. They may interact with human beings, either independently or on behalf of a deity.	Angels and demons are part of many religious traditions with diverse worldviews; there is no single description of the universe they occupy.
FANDOM	There are no overt views of the supernatural in fandom.	Human beings seek closeness to one another through shared ritual, mythology, culture, and experiences—which may all be achieved through fan communities. For some people, this closeness also has a spiritual dimension.	The imagined universe of fandom becomes reality through the devotion of community members. Often, themes in a particular movie or series illustrate deeper truths and suggest overall life strategies for fans.

NONRELIGIOUS BELIEFS

ATHEISM

INTRODUCTION

Atheism is a philosophical position which is based upon the assertion that no supreme, supernatural beings or forces exist. Instead, atheists contend that all phenomena in the universe, including human thought and morality, are products of nature and have no divine origin. Atheists also do not believe in the existence of a human soul which survives death.

HISTORY

Atheism is not exclusively a modern system of thought; more broadly, a diversity of traditions questioning the existence and significance of God has existed throughout history. Some Buddhist traditions are nontheistic, purporting that no divine intervention is needed to achieve human enlightenment. In ancient Greece, the sophists and Epicureans frequently challenged belief in the gods and divine action in the world, as did the philosopher Socrates. These philosophers did not completely deny the supernatural as much as they questioned religious political authority and the value of worshipping the gods for humanity. At the time of the Roman Empire, Christians were accused of atheism for the same reason—failing to accept the gods of the Empire as deserving worship. Additionally, during the Renaissance in Europe, a new type of humanism emerged in which people denied the religious realm as the only measure of excellence. However, none of these cases exactly mirror how atheism is defined today. Instead, these earlier understandings were a kind of skepticism and free thought which challenged the status quo. In contrast, modern atheists draw upon these same values but are more adamant in their ultimate denial of God.

BELIEFS

Modern atheism as a philosophical position has been profoundly influenced by the writings of Karl Marx, Sigmund Freud, and Friedrich Nietzsche. Each of these theorists saw Judeo-Christian religion in particular as a human creation, perhaps created out of necessity, which ultimately holds humanity back. Marx believed religion functioned like a drug to keep most people enslaved to the ruling class, Freud called religion an illusion, and Nietzsche famously asserted that God was dead. All three believed that atheism and a focus on the present were necessary to overcome human suffering and to release human potential. Jean-Paul Sartre added his support to the atheistic assertion of human freedom apart from belief in God.

Since 2008, there has been a rise in popular books about atheism, including works by authors like Christopher Hitchens and Richard Dawkins. These authors are often called "new atheists," and their approach moves beyond philosophy, as they encourage active resistance to religion in all its forms. They are concerned about how throughout history, religion has been used as a force of violence and oppression, and about how religious belief is built on superstition and denies scientific realities. Therefore, they assert that religion must be actively discredited. As a result, human morality will not be destroyed; rather, abandoning religion should enhance morality because it will no longer be based upon society's false and oppressive belief in God.

DEMOGRAPHICS

According to a recent Pew Forum survey, almost two percent of Americans identify themselves as atheists. Additionally, in the American Religious Identification Survey, conducted in 2008, as many as fifteen percent of Americans identified their religion as "none." Because this category includes atheists, agnostics, and other unaffiliated persons, the ARIS poll may not give accurate numbers of atheists specifically. However, it does give clues about how many Americans claim identities that do not hinge upon a belief in God.

FOR FURTHER READING

ARIS. "American Religious Identification Survey (ARIS 2008)." http://commons.trincoll.edu/aris/files/2011/08/ARIS_Report_2008.pdf

Dawkins, Richard. *The God Delusion*. Bantam Press: London, 2006.

Hitchens, Christopher. *God Is Not Great: How Religion Poisons Everything*. Hatchette Books: New York, 2007.

Pew Forum on Religion and Public Life. "Not All Nonbelievers Call Themselves Atheists." http://pewforum.org/Not-All-Nonbelievers-Call-Themselves-Atheists.aspx.

Thrower, James. *Western Atheism: A Short Introduction*. Prometheus Books: New York, 1971.

AGNOSTICISM

INTRODUCTION

Agnosticism is a philosophical position in which proponents are skeptical of the existence of a divine being, stating that it is impossible to prove using human reason. "Agnostic" literally means "not knowing" or "unknowable," and it is different from atheism, as atheists explicitly assert that divine beings do not exist.

HISTORY

Agnostics make no specific claim about the reality of a supernatural realm or of any deities. In the eighteenth and nineteenth centuries, David Hume, Immanuel Kant, and Soren Kierkegaard were skeptical of any claims for proof of the existence of God. However, it was T. H. Huxley in the 1860s who coined the term "agnostic." Because agnosticism is a category of not-knowing rather than a specific set of beliefs, it is not easily defined. For example, in 2008, the U.S. Religious Landscape Survey indicated that fifty-five percent of self-identified agnostics expressed a belief in God, and seventeen percent suggested they were "absolutely certain" that God or a universal spirit exists. In other words, a person may clearly believe in God but may still be agnostic, not drawing any conclusions about that God or making connections to any religion in particular.

Unlike agnosticism, "unaffiliated" as a category of religious belief does not have any specific history. Instead, it is a designation employed by polling organizations in response to an increasing dissatisfaction with organized religion. Being unaffiliated is essentially a catch-all category, including atheists, agnostics, and others who currently profess to be unassociated with any established religious tradition.

DEMOGRAPHICS

In a 2007 Pew Forum Survey, 2.4 percent of Americans describe themselves as agnostic. A much larger percent of the population (12.1 percent) respond that they are unaffiliated in either a "secular unaffiliated" (6.3 percent) or "religious unaffiliated" (5.8 percent) category. This category, also described as "nothing in particular," is the fastest growing group. Eighteen to twenty-nine year olds constitute the largest group of unaffiliated people in the United States, accounting for nearly one in four respondents.

According to the 2008 American Religious Identification Survey (ARIS), approximately 15 percent of Americans categorize their religion as "none," which includes both agnosticism and atheism. Additionally, 4.3 percent claim that there is "no way to know" if God exists. The "none" category also has the largest gender imbalance, with 60 percent being male.

FOR FURTHER READING

Kosmin, Barry A. and Ariela Keysar. "The American Religious Identification Survey (ARIS 2008)." http://commons.trincoll.edu/aris/files/2011/08/ARIS_Report_2008.pdf.

Pew Forum on Religion and Public Life. "U.S. Religious Landscape Survey." http://religions.pewforum.org/pdf/report-religious-landscape -study-key-findings.pdf.

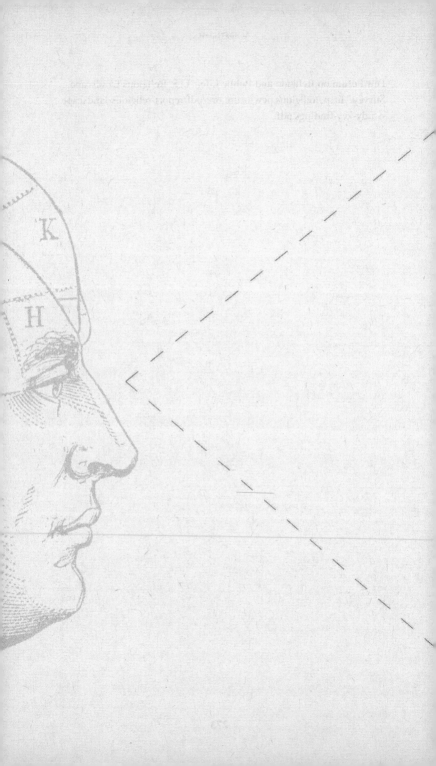

Postmodernism

INTRODUCTION

Postmodernism is a philosophical system that critiques the scientific, linguistic, and theoretical certainty of the rationality and modernism that developed during the Enlightenment.

Postmodernism traces its origins to the works of a handful of French philosophers, but has influenced discussions beyond philosophy including art, history, literature, political theory, popular culture, religion, and many more. Postmodernist ideals and ways of knowing are quite diverse, and sometimes contradictory. The key ideas of postmodernism have a broad impact on the world today.

HISTORY

To understand postmodernism, a person must first understand modernism, a term that is understood differently by different people depending on individual understandings of history, philosophy, and epistemology. Modernism arose from Enlightenment rationality. During and after World War II, modernists saw a European world in which Western scientific inquiry could produce real gains in human control over nature and in the ordering of culture. Having an optimistic belief in human progress, Modernists assumed that there were universal, real, and available answers to the questions of human existence, and that through science and rationality, Truth could be uncovered. In terms of human language, modernists believed that our words point to "real" ideas or have universal content; that is, when we talk, our words refer to static objects that have fixed meaning.

Beginning early in the twentieth century, philosophers began to question this unscrutinized faith in progress, truth, and universal meaning. Jean-Francois Lyotard, Jacques Derrida, and Michele Foucault were among the most famous critics of modernism, but it was Lyotard who brought postmodernism to the wider public in his 1979 work *The Postmodern Condition*. Lyotard's main critique is of what he calls metanarratives: all-encompassing, universal ideas that appear to be true for all people everywhere. Big ideas like progress or truth are actually attempts by the powers-that-be to legitimize their own perspectives, according to Lyotard. The poor, oppressed, and devalued in society get to neither create nor participate in these interpretations of events, but they are still expected to view them as somehow true. Lyotard (1984) uses the example of Auschwitz; in the Holocaust, progress and science were invoked by the Nazis to legitimize the extermination of entire peoples. In a post-Auschwitz world, then, we must approach this same type of language with skepticism, both in the present day and throughout history.

BELIEFS

The postmodernist opposition to modernist thought helps to define postmodernist beliefs. To appropriately critique modernist metanarratives, postmodernists sometimes employ a method known as deconstruction, made famous by Jacques Derrida in his work *Of Grammatology*. Derrida contended that our words—the words that modernists believed accurately described reality and mediated truth—are actually fraught with a diversity of competing meanings. Some of these meanings are given preferential status, while others are marginalized. This is the way metanarratives appear natural or universal—by giving authority to one meaning over another until that meaning appears to be true. By approaching with suspicion the authority structures of our language, we can dismantle their power and see instead that meaning is a changeable, unsubstantiated, and ultimately unstable product of culture, rather than a complete and stable whole. For example, a postmodernist critic of the Bible might question how the language of dominion in Genesis might legitimate a world in which humans see themselves as forces opposed to nature, a relationship that privileges humans. Recognizing this hierarchy allows the postmodernist to see this relationship between the earth and humans as only one possibility among many, rather than as the natural, obvious, or true way of viewing the world.

If all of this seems confusing, in some sense that confusion is among the aims of postmodernism. Postmodernist theorists want people to see the world as more complex than modernists believed it to be. In postmodernism, there is no universal truth, no scientific certainty, and no progress toward an ultimate utopian goal; instead, there is complexity in the competing meanings of words and ideas, and structures that must be resisted lest they become forces of oppression. To do so, people must always be suspicious of language, linear thinking, and claims of truth, and this may be where postmodernism has had its greatest impact on present-day society. In the popular postmodern world, people talk about individual truth, and are suspicious of claims to ultimate truth. Reading hypertext online often replaces reading linear history in a book. Furthermore, people use images and symbols in diverse ways, usually without trying to connect them to an original meaning. Think about Lady Gaga singing about Judas as her lover in the song *Judas*, for example. All of these ways of thinking and being are part of the postmodernist impact on people's lives.

FOR FURTHER READING

Butler, Christopher. *Postmodernism: A Very Short Introduction*. (Oxford: Oxford University Press, 2003).

Lyotard, Jean-Francois. *The Postmodern Condition: A Report on Knowledge*. (Minneapolis: University of Minnesota Press, 1984).

SECULAR HUMANISM

INTRODUCTION

Secular Humanism is a twentieth-century, nonreligious philosophy that looks to science and sensory experience to determine human understanding and morality. It denounces any religious worldview, including the existence of a divine being—God or otherwise—and the reality of the supernatural.

HISTORY

Humanism, defined broadly, is a philosophical position that values human ways of understanding, especially when it comes to determining truth. Humanists tend to appeal to reason, scientific inquiry, and/or natural consequences in establishing morality and goodness. The humanist tradition has roots in ancient Greek thought, particularly its emphasis on rationality and inquisitiveness. Humanist principles were significant in Renaissance and Reformation Europe, since both periods stressed the role of the individual in distinguishing truth from untruth rather than relying on church teachings. The humanist tradition also draws upon the skepticism and democratic principles of the eighteenth century Enlightenment. Therefore, by definition the humanist tradition is not exclusively secular, but rather humanism is simply a philosophical position that affirms the importance of human faculties in determining truth and decency. Secular Humanism grew out of this larger humanist movement, and became a unique phenomenon with the publication of the *Humanist Manifesto* in 1933 and the subsequent *Secular Humanist Declaration* in 1980.

BELIEFS

Secular Humanists do not affirm the existence of any god or transcendent realm. However, Secular Humanism is not simply atheism. Atheism is a denial of the existence of any god, whereas Secular Humanism expands beyond simple denial and offers a positive system of values. Paul Kurtz, one of the most famous advocates of Secular Humanism, stated, "The main thrust of humanism is not to simply espouse the negative, what we do *not* believe in, but what we *do*. I am a secular humanist because I am not religious. I draw my inspiration not from religion or spirituality, but from science, ethics, philosophy, and the arts" (2008). In other words, Secular Humanists seek the separation of the religious from civic matters, the endorsement of free thinking, and the affirmation of human responsibility in both creating and solving world problems, rather than blaming sin and hoping for divine salvation (see the "Affirmations" page at www.secularhumanism.org).

Some people might challenge Secular Humanism's being defined as a "religion" because it lacks any sense of a supernatural realm and does not seek transcendent sources for morality; therefore, better terminology for this movement might be "philosophy" or "worldview." However, Secular Humanism was classified as a nontheistic religion in the Supreme Court opinion *Torcaso v. Watkins* in 1961. Creationists who oppose Secular Humanism's commitment to evolution have also described it as a religion, and often see it as a threat to Christian beliefs. For example, the Conservative Christian author Homer Duncan titled his book on the subject *Secular Humanism: The Most Dangerous Religion in America*.

DEMOGRAPHICS

It is difficult to pinpoint the exact number of Secular Humanists in the world. Many secular humanists live in cultures in which they may be reluctant to define themselves as such. For example, in some nations where religion is state sponsored, Secular Humanists could be punished by death. It has been suggested that approximately ten percent of the population of any nation could be defined as Secular Humanist. However, it is almost impossible to know for sure.

FOR FURTHER READING

Council for Secular Humanism. http://www.secularhumanism.org/.

Kurtz, Paul. "The Convictions of a Humanist." *Humanist* 68.3 (2008): 21–25.

NONRELIGIOUS BELIEFS COMPARED TO CHRISTIANITY

	NATURE OF THE SUPERNATURAL	NATURE OF HUMANITY	NATURE OF THE UNIVERSE
CHRISTIANITY	One creator-God in three persons: Father, Son, and Holy Spirit. God is personal, interacts with humanity, is all-knowing, and all-powerful.	God allows humans free will to choose between right and wrong. However, they are inherently sinful and are incapable of achieving salvation on their own. Ultimately, salvation only comes through God.	This world is temporary. We are engaged in a battle between good and evil. Someday God will judge all people at the end of time, which will bring the long-awaited coming of the "Kingdom of God."
ATHEISM	Atheists insist that no deities or other supernatural forces exist.	Human beings have no soul which survives death. Present life in the material world is the full extent of human existence.	The universe is not the creation of a higher power, but instead is purely the product of nature.
AGNOSTICISM	Existence of deities and supernatural forces is viewed with skepticism.	There are limits to human logic and ability. Human beings are incapable of understanding essential truths about God, religion, and the universe.	It is impossible to know about the universe using human reason.
POSTMODERNISM	Ideas about God and the supernatural are merely human constructions.	Human beings often restrict themselves to conventional forms of knowledge, whereas postmodernism allows people to consider the full range of possibilities. People should view all things with skepticism because human understanding is subjective and not objective.	Humans construct the universe and then view that as "real." There are no essential truths, since truth is socially determined. The universe need not be restricted by people's need to cling to comfortable ways of knowing.
SECULAR HUMANISM	Human knowledge and understanding takes the place of any higher power.	Human ways of understanding truth through reason and scientific inquiry are celebrated; personal responsibility and free thought are encouraged. Rather than relying on external direction, secular humanists rely on their own internal sense of right and wrong.	The universe is knowable through science and sensory experience. With a lack of focus on any supernatural realm, the emphasis is on the physical world—knowing it scientifically, and acting in it responsibly.

EXTREMISM

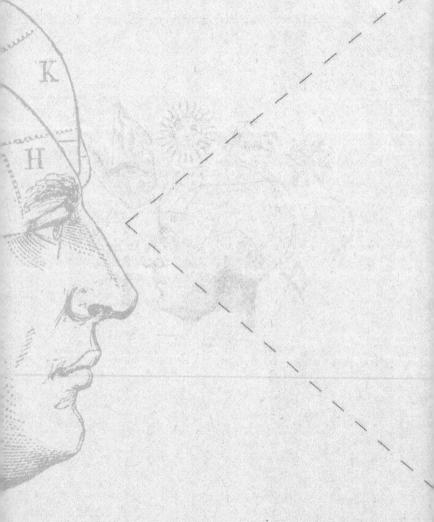

FUNDAMENTALISM

INTRODUCTION

Fundamentalism refers to the idea that a given political or religious doctrine should be taken literally, neither interpreted nor adapted in any way. Religious fundamentalism does not apply to any single tradition; rather, it is a term used for a wide variety of traditions which share common principles. Usually, fundamentalists believe that their religious texts and authorities are without error, see their faith as a unique means of salvation, and view modernity as a threat to their traditional beliefs and practices. Recently, fundamentalism has expanded beyond religious issues and has embraced political positions and nationalist ideals. While fundamentalism began in the United States and was originally associated with a particular type of Protestant Christianity, more recently the term has been applied to groups within other religions, including Islam, Judaism, and Hinduism.

CHRISTIAN FUNDAMENTALISM

Fundamentalism originally referred to a type of Christianity that developed in the United States at the beginning of the twentieth century. This form of Christianity was essentially reactionary, based on a perceived threat from liberalism, biblical criticism which challenged Mosaic authorship of the Torah, and the emergence of scientific principles like evolution that challenged God as creator of the universe. In response, a group of Protestant clergy and laypeople wrote *The Fundamentals: A Testimony to the Truth*, which became the basis for Christian fundamentalism; foremost among the beliefs these authors expressed was the claim that the words of the Bible were inerrant, being the literal words of God. From this central claim, fundamentalists rejected higher biblical criticism; asserted the literal virgin birth, resurrection, and return of Jesus; and denied the possibility of evolution in the creation of humanity. The authors of *The Fundamentals* also railed against the perceived threats of socialism, Catholicism, Mormonism, and Christian Science. Protestant institutions of higher learning, including Princeton Seminary and Moody Bible College, were especially important to the dissemination of fundamentalist ideals, and believed their students to be training to defend conservatism.

More recently, fundamentalist Christianity in the United States has become not only a religious force but a political force as well. The same fears of liberalism and modernity, and the same commitment to biblical literalism, especially related to social issues, led to the rise of the Christian Right in the 1970s and 80s. The Christian Right is a term that refers to "right-wing" Christians who generally support socially conservative policies, citing religious texts as justification for their political beliefs. In the 70s and 80s, the Christian Right sought to respond to perceived threats to their traditional beliefs with political activism as well as religious training. The Reverend Jerry Falwell's Moral Majority, founded in 1979, is widely seen as the first Christian Right group to take this approach. Additionally, Pat Robertson's Christian Coalition and the anti-abortion group Operation Rescue exerted enormous influence in 1990s politics, finding particularly strong allies within the Republican Party.

The modern political wing of Christian fundamentalism has been influential in establishing a political platform that opposes same-sex marriage, abortion, and contraception-based sex education. From these shared concerns, the originally Protestant movement has drawn a strong Catholic element. Modern fundamentalists have also challenged scientific consensus about climate change and opposed the teaching of evolution as a means for understanding human origins in biology courses.

In 2008, the Pew Forum on Religion and Public Life researched Christians belief and found that while only one percent of Christians identify their church membership as explicitly fundamentalist, in reality, fundamentalist principles are much more widespread. For example, twenty-two percent of mainline (not evangelical or fundamentalist) Christians believed that the Bible is "the Word of God, to be taken literally word for word." Comparatively, twenty-nine percent of mainline Christians completely disagreed that evolution best explains human origins (http://religions.pewforum.org/pdf/report-religious-landscape-study-full.pdf).

OTHER FORMS OF FUNDAMENTALISM

Other religious traditions have similar movements characterized by religious conservatism, textual literalism, and a rejection of modernity. Both scholars and the media refer to these groups as fundamentalists.

Islamic Fundamentalism

Islamic fundamentalism refers to Muslims who take the Qur'an (the holy scripture of Islam) and in some cases the Sunnah (the teachings and actions of Muhammad) literally, and who seek the establishment of Muslim states in an effort to best follow the demands of the Qur'an. The Iranian Revolution of 1979 was one of the most famous political expressions of Islamic fundamentalism. In this revolution, the Shah of Iran was replaced by the Ayatollah Khomeini, a religious revolutionary, to establish a theocracy, which is an explicitly religious government. Iran continues to be an Islamic republic and maintains strict enforcement of the religious law called the Sharia. Other Islamic fundamentalist groups include the Wahhabi of Saudi Arabia and the Taliban of Afghanistan.

Jewish Fundamentalism

Jewish fundamentalism also has both religious and political elements. Among the religious fundamentalists are the Haredim, also called Ultra-Orthodox Jews, who view both the written and oral Torah as God-given and absolutely authoritative in all matters of life. As such, strict observance of the Sabbath and kosher law are required. Dress is also conservative, and men and women worship separately to maintain community perceptions of modesty and propriety. Among Jewish political fundamentalists are those who want to hasten the messianic kingdom in Israel by occupying parts of the Holy Land given to Palestinians after World War II. Sometimes these Jews are called Zionists. One example of a political Zionist group is the Gush Emunim, established on the principles, "The Land of Israel, for the People of Israel, under the Torah of Israel." However, Zionism is not always a fundamentalist movement, so these terms should not be equated.

Hindu Fundamentalism

Fundamentalist sects also appear among Hindus in India. However, these movements focus less upon religious conservatism and more upon political goals. For example, proponents of the Hindutva and Vishva Hindu Parashad movements seek to establish India as a Hindu nation, and their focus is to promote religious nationalism. Whereas fundamentalists in Christianity, Judaism, and Islam often find themselves in conflict with non-fundamentalists in their own traditions, Hindu fundamentalists tend to promote pan-Hindu solidarity. As a result, conflict in Hindu fundamentalism is more likely to be directed at non-Hindus.

Fundamentalism in Public Life

Karen Armstrong, author of twelve books on comparative religion, has noted that one of the overriding emotions driving modern fundamentalism is a fear of change. Fundamentalists, whether religious or political, see societal changes as a threat to the traditional values and beliefs they hold dear, so they actively resist these changes. Sometimes this resistance is in the form of strict doctrinal controls, like the values expressed in

The Fundamentals or the strict enforcement of Sharia law. At other times resistance takes the form of political protest, as in the Moral Majority or the Iranian Revolution. A common thread, however, is a concern about a shifting society, a belief in the importance of maintaining traditional religious principles, and a commitment to live these principles in both religious and political spheres. All of these factors have contributed to the rise of fundamentalism in America and around the world.

FOR FURTHER READING

Abadi, Jacob. "Religious Zionism and Israeli Politics: Gush Emunim Revisited." Pages 67–90 in *Religious Fundamentalism in Developing Countries*. Santosh Saha and Thomas Karr, eds. Westport, CT: Greenwood Press, 2001.

Armstrong, Karen. *The Battle for God: A History of Fundamentalism*. New York: Random House, 2000.

Marty, Martin. *Fundamentalisms Observed*. Chicago: University of Chicago Press, 1994.

Pew Forum on Religion and Public Life. "U.S. Religious Landscape Survey." http://religions.pewforum.org/.

RELIGIOUS VIOLENCE

INTRODUCTION

According to scholar Mark Juergensmeyer, in 1980, "scarcely a single religious organization" was listed on the U.S. State Department's terrorism watch list. Twenty years later, over half of the organizations on the watch list were religiously affiliated. What accounts for the rise of religious violence? Has this tendency always existed in religions? Are religions violent by nature, or is religious violence the result of isolated persons who misinterpret their religions? This short chapter cannot address the full complexity of the topic of religious violence; however, it may provide some starting points for further discussion.

Violence is evident in many religions, including Judaism, Christianity, Islam, Hinduism, and Buddhism. Though many people may associate violence most powerfully with the Abrahamic religions, other religions are also not immune to religious justification for violent acts—even religions like Buddhism, which espouses the principle of ahimsa (nonviolence), and Hinduism, which people often associate with nonviolence and vegetarianism. In addition, smaller new religious movements have demonstrated that they, too, may have the potential for violence.

VIOLENCE IN ABRAHAMIC RELIGIONS

Jewish scriptures are sometimes used to justify violence; in fact, some parts of the Hebrew Bible offer quite graphic portrayals of hatred, murder, and war. When the Israelites take the land of Canaan, they are commanded to "utterly destroy" the inhabitants of the land (Deut.7:2). When the promised land is threatened, Israelite judges kill opposing armies in response (Judg. 3; 15). When the land is overthrown by the Babylonians, the exiled Israelites express hope that the Babylonian babies will have their heads smashed by rocks (Ps. 137). Then when they finally return, Esther and Mordecai are praised for plotting the death of Haman and his sons, an event which is celebrated to this day during Purim. Violence is not only related to national strife either; interpersonal violence happens between spouses (Lev. 19), parents and children (Judg. 11:37–39), and siblings (Gen. 4), all with religious motivations. God, too, is described as a warrior (Ex. 15:3), and even as an abusive husband (Ezek. 16).

In post-biblical Judaism, the Jewish people have been involved in violent religious conflicts with pagans, Christians, and Muslims. Jews under Roman rule refused to submit to what they considered idolatry, and they responded with violent rebellions like the Bar Kochba revolt. Elliott Horowitz has argued persuasively that in Judaism throughout history, responding to conflict with violent behavior has been justified by means of the Purim tale in which Jews kill their oppressors. Recently, Jewish groups have justified attacks on Palestinians by claiming rights to the land of Israel. For example, during the massacre at the Tomb of the Patriarchs in Hebron, twenty-nine Muslims were killed and more than one hundred wounded by a Brooklyn doctor who believed only Jewish people had a rightful claim to the Holy Land (http://www

.independent.co.uk/news/world/hebron-massacre-brooklyn
-doctor-with-a-prescription-for-hatred-1396680.html).

In Christianity, New Testament authors also often
employ violent imagery. Jesus claims in the Gospel of
Matthew that he came "not to bring peace, but a sword"
(10:36), and to set members of families against each other
for the sake of the faith. The unfaithful will "suffer the
punishment of eternal destruction" by flaming angels,
according to the writer of 2 Thessalonians. Additionally,
in the book of Revelation, humanity is pressed into a
winepress, and blood flows as "high as a horse's bridle,
for a distance of about two hundred miles" on the Day of
Judgment (14:20).

Images like these informed Christian attitudes
throughout following centuries, and were often invoked
to justify acts of violence against others, particularly
non-Christians. John Collins has noted the way in which
Christians used the Bible to support the Crusades, the
Puritan revolt in England, the mistreatment of Native
Americans in the United States, and many apocalyptic
movements in Europe and America. Slave owners
in pre-Civil War America regularly justified their
violence toward slaves with quotes from the epistles,
stating, "Slaves submit to your masters" (1 Peter 2:18).
Furthermore, misinterpretation of who is to blame for
the crucifixion has resulted in rampant anti-Semitism,
including justification for the Holocaust. Today, Christian
extremist groups continue to justify their violence as
faithfulness to God and to the Bible. For example, the
anti-abortion beliefs of Presbyterian minister Paul Hill
led him to murder a women's health doctor named John

Britton in 1994. In 2010, members of the Hutaree militia group of Michigan were arrested for devising a plot to kill police officers in an effort to bring about the Apocalypse.

As in Jewish and Christian scriptures, violent imagery also appears in the Qur'an. For example, in surah 5, a warning is given to "those who wage war against Allah and his people . . . that they should be murdered or crucified, or their hands and their feet should be cut off" (5:33). In surah 9, believers are encouraged to "slay the idolaters wherever you find them," and in surah 33, hypocrites and agitators are warned that "wherever they are found, they shall be seized and murdered" (33:61). However, the often quoted text promising virgins to those who martyr themselves is not actually about martyrs at all, but is instead a vision of paradise for all the faithful (56:10–38). In spite of this fact, some extremists have still used this text to encourage terrorism.

In modern times, acts of terrorism by Islamic extremist groups have received significant attention in both scholarship and the media. In 1972, Palestinian extremists kidnapped and killed Israeli athletes at the Olympic Games. Then in 1979, Iranian students who supported the Shi'ite Ayatollah seized the United States Embassy and took 66 hostages, resulting in a standoff that lasted 444 days. Additionally, more than 240 Marines were killed in Beirut, Lebanon in 1983, an attack carried out by the radical Shi'ite group Hezbollah. Then under the auspices of reestablishing a Muslim state, the terrorist group al-Qaeda has perpetrated attacks in Kenya, Tanzania, Somalia, and Yemen; they are also purported to be behind the attack on the U.S.S. Cole in 2000 and the September 11, 2001, attacks on New York City and Washington, DC. Furthermore, in India, Pakistani Muslim groups have been responsible for the deaths of thousands of Kashmiri Hindus in an attempt at ethnic cleansing resulting from territory disputes.

Of course, extremism, hatred, and violence are present in practically all religions, though no religion is universally violent. Also, sometimes violence that is justified with religious language is actually motivated by political or economic factors. However, each person must bear responsibility for his or her own violent actions, recognizing that these actions reflect badly upon the overall religion. Furthermore, this chapter primarily addresses organized acts of collective violence, but on an individual level, interpersonal violence and intolerance can also have religious motivations. For example, violence against women, child abuse, and homophobia can all result from religious beliefs, even among non-extremists.

VIOLENCE IN ASIAN RELIGIONS

Though many people stereotypically view Asian religions as more peaceful traditions, both Hinduism and Buddhism also have some violent elements. In these contexts, there are political and nationalist components that feed religious violence.

Violent Hindu nationalism is most obvious in the ongoing conflict between India and Pakistan. During the partition of India after liberation from British rule in 1947, the states of East and West Pakistan were created; East Pakistan eventually became Bangladesh in 1971. The division was largely religious, with India being primarily

Hindu and Pakistan primarily Muslim. This partition resulted in significant violence, as both Hindus and Muslims felt as if they were being forced to relocate their families based upon their religious identities; this fostered deep resentment between the two groups. As a result, the relocation process itself was extremely dangerous, with violence frequently erupting between Hindus and Muslims en route. Estimates are that as many as a million people were killed during that summer. For a graphic but important look at partition violence, see BBC News photographs at http://news.bbc.co.uk/2/shared/spl/hi/pop _ups/06/south_asia_india0s_partition/html/5.stm. Today, parts of the northern territory of Kashmir, which lies on the border between India and Pakistan, continue to be disputed.

In 1992, Hindu nationalists destroyed the Babri Mosque, which dated back to the 1500s, in the city of Ayodhya. Hindus believed that the mosque was built over the birthplace of Lord Ram, who is an avatar of Vishnu and the beloved hero of the Ramayana, a famous religious epic. Both Hindus and Muslims claimed the same ground as sacred, resulting in an ongoing dispute that lasted over a hundred years. Unfortunately, the eventual outcome was violent conflict; the mosque was razed, and over 2,000 Hindus and Muslims were killed during the attack and associated riots throughout India and Pakistan. Violence also erupted in Gujarat province in 2002 after Muslims bombed a train filled with Hindus who had been on a pilgrimage to Ayodhya, and who were finally returning home. Fifty-nine men, women, and children were killed in this attack, and in response, Hindu mobs killed close to 800 Muslims and torched Islamic places of worship. Around 250 Hindus also died during these riots. These two examples of inter-religious conflicts are the result not only of religious divisions but also of political divisions. Because religious identity is so tied to national identity, the religious and the political are practically inseparable, which only escalates the potential for conflict.

Though images of a peacefully meditating Buddha and untroubled monks are commonplace in Buddhism, this tradition is also not immune to conflict. Buddhism has a history of violence and political conquest, from encouraging assassination in Tibet to the violent, gun-wielding tactics of Buddhist military monks in Thailand (see Jerryson and Juergensmeyer). Buddhist nationalism has been the force behind clashes in Sri Lanka involving violence between the Buddhist majority population and the minority Tamils, who are primarily Hindu and Christian, over the creation of a Tamil homeland. This conflict led to a twenty-six-year civil war, finally ending in 2009 with the victory of the Sri Lankan military and the defeat of the Tamil insurgents. Some estimates are that as many as 100,000 people were killed on both sides combined.

NEW RELIGIOUS MOVEMENTS AND VIOLENCE

While new religious movements are not all violent in nature, there are examples of some groups becoming violent or even deadly. If there exists the influence of a powerful leader, coupled with isolation from the outside world, there can be devastating results.

In 1993, the U.S. Bureau of Alcohol, Tobacco, and Firearms (ATF) entered a standoff with the Branch Davidians of Mt. Carmel outside of Waco, Texas. The leader of this group, David Koresh, was convinced for years that the members of the compound were preparing for an apocalyptic battle, based on his reading of the Revelation. He saw himself as the messiah in this coming war, and believed he had a responsibility to raise up an army by fathering children with the women of the community—a belief he called the New Light Doctrine— and by actively recruiting new members. In preparation for the battle, the Branch Davidians had been stockpiling weapons. The initial stage of the 1993 standoff, which left several ATF agents and group members dead, only intensified Koresh's belief that the end of days was upon them. It is unclear whether the Davidians would have actually used their weapons had they been pushed further; the standoff came to a disturbing end when a fire engulfed the compound and killed most of the people inside. Upon investigating the incident, the Danforth Commission (an independent, government-appointed panel) indicated that the Branch Davidians themselves might have started the fire, perhaps to take their own lives rather than submit to an authority they believed to be the anti-Christ.

Similarly violent suicides under the leadership of charismatic individuals have taken place elsewhere. One well-known example took place in Jonestown, Guyana, where the Reverend Jim Jones and his associates convinced more than 900 members of the People's Temple to end their own lives and take the lives of their children with cyanide rather than submit to an investigation by U.S.

Congressman Leo Ryan in 1978. Congressman Ryan was assassinated during his investigation. Another incident occurred in San Diego, California in 1997, when Marshall Applewhite convinced thirty-eight followers to end their own lives so that they might access a UFO they believed was trailing a comet. The members of the cult, called Heaven's Gate, called the process of taking their own lives "membership in the Next Level," an indication of their belief that this life was only one plane of existence.

Rarely, cults have also acted homicidally, as was the case with the Charles Manson Family in 1969. Manson was able to gather followers from the California counter-culture movement, who would eventually murder on his behalf, by claiming that he was the second coming of Jesus and that the murders were necessary to spark a race riot that would lead to Armageddon. Thirty years later, members of the Movement for the Restoration of the Ten Commandments stabbed, strangled, and bludgeoned hundreds of Ugandans who were critical of the movement and who refused to adhere to the Ten Commandments, according to what group members believed. Additionally, in 1994–95, dozens were killed and thousands injured in poison gas attacks in Japan, perpetrated by a group called Aum Shinrikyo in response to perceived political and social threats in Japan.

Usually, violence committed by cult groups is precipitated by a sense of apocalyptic or millennial expectation, and/or oppression or mistreatment at the hands of the larger culture. A galvanizing figure often plays a role in instigating the violence, though she or he does not always personally commit the acts.

IS RELIGION A FORCE FOR VIOLENCE?

No religious tradition, large or small, is safe from violent tendencies. Observing widespread religious hatred has led anti-religion writers like atheist author Christopher Hitchens to proclaim that "religion poisons everything." Furthermore, even people who believe religion can be a force for good must admit that the actions of people in the name of religion, as well as the rhetoric of religious texts, have been damaging, destructive, and traumatic. It is unfair to those who have been traumatized by religious violence to gloss over their hurt by downplaying religion's role in their trauma. Instead, we must investigate the extremism and anger that has fostered religious violence and begin to think and act in ways that counter those harmful elements. If religion can be a force for violence, then it can also be a force for good.

FOR FURTHER READING

Bromley, David G. and J. Gordon Melton, eds. *Cults, Religion, and Violence*. Oxford: Oxford University Press, 2002.

Brown, Robert McAfee. *Religion and Violence*. Philadelphia: Westminster Press, 1987.

Burns, Charlene Embrey. *More Moral Than God: Taking Responsibility for Religious Violence*. Lanham, MD: Rowman and Littlefield: 2008.

Collins, John J. *Does the Bible Justify Violence?* Minneapolis: Augsburg Fortress, 2004.

Hagerty, Barbara Bradley. "Is the Bible More Violent Than the Koran?" NPR News. March 18, 2010.

Horowitz, Elliot. *Reckless Rites: Purim and the Legacy of Jewish Violence*. Princeton: Princeton University Press, 2006.

Jerryson, Michael and Mark Juergensmeyer. *Buddhist Warfare*. Oxford: Oxford University Press, 2009.

Juergensmeyer, Mark. *Terror in the Mind of God: The Global Rise of Religious Violence*. Berkeley: University of California Press, 2003.

Repp, Martin. "Religion and Violence in Japan." Pages 147–72 in *Violence and New Religious Movements*. James R. Lewis, ed. Oxford: Oxford University Press, 2011.

Walliss, John. *Apocalyptic Trajectories: Millenarianism and Violence in the Contemporary World*. Bern: European Academic Publishers, 2004.

Warraq, Ibn. "Virgins? What Virgins?" *The Guardian* (January 11, 2002).

*Mayan calendar
carved out of bone*

APOCALYPTICISM

INTRODUCTION

Apocalypticism is a belief in the impending end of
the world or of this age, often in conjunction with the
arrival of a messiah or prophet who will judge humanity
at the end of time, or eschaton. Most people professing
apocalyptic beliefs hold a linear cosmology—a view of
the universe in which all things exist on a single timeline,
rather than in an endlessly recycling world—and a
profound sense of cosmological dualism, in which there
exists a battle of good versus evil. While apocalyptic
beliefs are most often associated with religions like
Judaism, Zoroastrianism, Christianity, and Islam, popular
apocalypticism has proliferated and moved beyond these
earliest iterations. Since these first ancient apocalyptic
pronouncements, so-called prophets have repeatedly
claimed an imminent end of the world. Recently,
apocalyptic paranoia has been manifested in the 2012
Mayan calendar phenomenon, among others.

HISTORY

Ancient Apocalypticism

Apocalypticism, as a way of seeing the world, grew
out of the political climate of the Greek and Roman
empires. Both empires were oppressive toward non-
dominant religions (Judaism under the Greeks, or
Judaism and Christianity under the Romans). They
demanded obedience to the empire and the renunciation

of monotheistic beliefs and practices. Imperial armies and puppet kings often interfered in the functioning of the Temple in Jerusalem, defiling it with pagan sacrifices. Under such despotic rule, the oppressed began to question whether God had abandoned them, even though they had been faithful.

The genre of apocalyptic literature is a response to this oppression and the theological questions it raises. Broadly, apocalyptic literature is:

1. Cosmic in scope, meaning it sees current oppressors as a part of a larger universal battle for ultimate authority;

2. Dualistic, meaning it divides all people and powers into two camps—good or evil—as well as anticipating a dualistic judgment to eternal life or damnation;

3. Eschatological, or concerned with the end of this age;

4. Allegorical or symbolic, with images or words standing in for other ideas, people, or things; and

5. Revealed, usually by a divine agent, angel, or messianic figure.

By creating a style of literature that uses veiled images and coded, symbolic language, apocalyptic authors were able to speak about the coming end of oppression and the in-breaking reign of God without fear of persecution by reigning governments. In this way, they were able to manage their situations as oppressed peoples, believing the world would soon come to an end and the evildoers would be punished. The Apocalypse of Enoch, the Book of Daniel chapters 7–12, Mark 13, and Revelation are among the many examples of Jewish and Christian apocalyptic literature from the Greco-Roman period.

The holy text of Islam, known as the Qur'an, emerged five centuries later and shares many of the apocalyptic features found in Judeo-Christian texts. Several chapters, or surahs, of the Qur'an emphasize a coming judgment of humanity, a resurrection of the body to either eternal life or eternal torment, and an end of the current age (see surahs 22, 39, 40, and 82). In the hundred years after the completion of the Qur'an, Muslims developed the concept of the Mahdi, a redeemer who will usher in the final judgment; this idea is especially prominent among Shi'ites.

Later Apocalypticism

For a few centuries after the legalization of Christianity, apocalypticism waned among Christians. However, with the rapid spread of Islam, Christians in Europe began to wonder if the new religion was a sign of the coming end of the world. That fear was magnified when Muslims expanded into Jerusalem. In addition, the mention of a thousand-year reign of Christ in the Apocalypse of John led some people to believe that the final battle was theirs to fight as the millennium approached. Particularly in England and France, preachers, monks, and writers stoked this fear, though there is no scholarly consensus on how great the level of panic was throughout other parts of Europe. For example, Bernard of Thuringia, a well-known hermit, predicted the world would end in 992, and Adso of Montier-en-Dur, writing in 950, vividly described the soon-to-come antichrist in a letter to Queen Gerbera of France. Sylvester II, Pope during the year 1000, did not mention the apocalypse in his own writing, and dismissed with a blessing the fearful gathering in Rome on the eve of the millennium when the dreaded end did not arrive.

However, the passing of the year 1000 did not end apocalyptic expectations. In Judaism, Kabbalistic mystics used astrological charts to predict the imminent arrival of the messiah and the redemption of the Jewish people in texts like the *Zohar*. Building upon these expectations, the Jewish mystic Shabbatai Zevi claimed to be the long-awaited messiah, anticipating the apocalypse in 1666 (see Himmelfarb). Moshe Edel has suggested that, like its ancient apocalyptic counterparts, Jewish apocalyptic writing post-1000 CE was still inspired by oppression, this time at the hands of European Christians. Similarly, Muslims developed astrologically oriented apocalyptic writings in the eleventh and twelfth centuries, in response to the Crusades and the Mongol invasions. While apparently not motivated by political fears, Christian mystics like Hildegard of Bingen wrote about graphic apocalyptic visions during this time as well.

It would be impossible to trace the breadth of apocalyptic movements over the next 900 years, given the sheer volume of examples. However, a few from American religious history deserve mention. Christian apocalyptic fervor in the New World was evident early on. For example, Christopher Columbus called himself "the messenger of the new heaven and the new earth" when reflecting on his "discovery" of the Americas (see Stein). The Puritans, too, saw themselves as part of the fulfillment of the eschatological kingdom, referring to their city as a New Jerusalem. One hundred years later in the American colonies, fiery preachers like Jonathan Edwards brought about the Great Awakening, which is characterized by religious revivalism and claims that the end of the world was soon to come. Additionally, under the leadership of Joseph Smith, people in the new Mormon movement in the 1830s called themselves Latter-day Saints, believing they were living in the last days. During the same decade, a farmer named William Miller convinced hundreds of people that the world would end in 1843 and, subsequently, 1844. As a result, the date October 22, 1844—the date predicted by Millerite preacher Samuel Snow—became known as the Great Disappointment because of the thousands of people who waited in vain for the end to arrive. Events of the later nineteenth and twentieth centuries, particularly the Civil War and World Wars I and II, also fueled apocalyptic expectation.

As the second millennium came to an end, the late twentieth century saw renewed apocalyptic fervor. Conservative Christian writers like Hal Lindsey (*Late Great Planet Earth*), Tim Lahaye, and Jerry Jenkins (The *Left Behind* series) told stories of biblical apocalypse to modern audiences, and their books became bestsellers. These books also fueled the discussion among fundamentalist Christian circles about premillennial, amillennial, and postmillennial views of the apocalypse (see Boch). In Judaism, Hasidic Chabad–Lubavitch groups in Brooklyn, New York claimed that Rabbi Menachem

Mendel Schneerson was the messiah on earth, here to redeem the world.

Small, separatist Christian sects isolated themselves and prepared for the coming apocalypse, often with disastrous results. For example, the Branch Davidians were an offshoot of the Seventh-Day Adventists, growing out of the Millerite movement of the 1800s. Believing David Koresh's expectations of Christ's return, the Branch Davidians secluded themselves inside a Waco, Texas compound and ended up facing off with the government, resulting in the deaths of over eighty people. Another tragic example of an apocalyptic group is the People's Temple, begun by Jim Jones in California, who eventually moved the group to Guyana in order to establish a utopic community called Jonestown. The People's Temple ended in a combination of murder and mass suicide in 1978, when over 900 men, women, and children died at Jones's command. In these cases, public reaction varied radically. Documentaries like William Gazecki's *Waco: Rules of Engagement* actually presents the Branch Davidians in a positive way and blames the government for their demise. Stanley Nelson's *Jonestown: The Life and Death of the People's Temple*, on the other hand, presents a very negative view of Jim Jones. The syncretic religious group Heaven's Gate also predicted a sort of alien apocalypse, as they awaited a UFO following the Hale-Bopp comet in 1997. Again, there were tragic consequences as thirty-nine members of this group took their own lives in order to unite with the spacecraft.

The advent of the year 2000 (Y2K) led to additional apocalyptic predictions, this time with a technological spin, with computers playing a key role in the approaching end. Then when the world did not end in the year 2000, an obscure interpretation of the Mayan calendar became the new focus of end-times predictions. According to proponents, the Mayan Long Count calendar should reset on December 21, 2012, based on cyclical eras of approximately 394 years, and this will usher in the end of the current age. The planets will align, causing cosmic devastation. However, as Krupp and many others have explained, the Long Count calendar does not portend cataclysmic events, nor will the planets align in any substantive way. Further, the Maya saw many cyclical eras beyond the end of the current cycle, indicating they did not view the coming 2012 date as the "end of the world."

WHY APOCALYPTICISM MATTERS

In an opinion piece for the *New Scientist*, Michael Shermer reiterated what has been apparent since the beginnings of apocalypticism: "Apocalyptic visions . . . help us make sense of an often seemingly senseless world. In the face of confusion and annihilation, we need restitution and reassurance." Indeed, throughout time, apocalypticism has helped those who fear the world around them to be reassured that the chaos was soon to end. Just as Jewish people sought the messianic age to escape subjugation, and as Christians used numerology and scripture to assuage their fears of a looming Muslim invasion, today's apocalyptic movements often see the end of the world as a new beginning. This worldview allows the oppressed to look forward to their freedom, and the religious to look forward to their ultimate reward. Apocalyptic worldviews depict a world in which current injustices are righted, allowing the human mind to find patterns in apparently senseless world events. Given these spiritual, political, and psychological benefits, we are unlikely to have seen the end of apocalypticism.

FOR FURTHER READING

Bock, Darrell L., ed. *Three Views on the Millennium and Beyond.* Grand Rapids: Zondervan, 1999.

Edel, Moshe. "Jewish Apocalypticism: 670–1670." Pages 354–79 in *The Continuum History of Apocalypticism.* Bernard McGinn, John J. Collins, and Stephen J. Stein, eds. New York: Continuum, 2003.

Himmelfarb, Martha. *The Apocalypse: A Brief History.* Oxford: Blackwell, 2010.

Krupp, E.C. "The 2012 Scare." *Sky and Telescope.* 118.5 (2009) 22–26.

Landes, Richard Allen, Andrew Gow and David Van Meter, eds. *The Apocalyptic Year 1000: Religious Expectation and Social Change, 950 to 1050.* Oxford: Oxford University Press, 2003.

Shermer, Michael. "The End is Always Nigh." *New Scientist* 210.2815 (2011) 30–31.

Stein, Stephen J. "American Millennial Visions: Towards Constructions of a New Architectonic of American Apocalypticism." Pages 187–233 in *Imagining the End: Visions of Apocalypse from the Ancient Middle East to Modern America.* Abbas Amanat and Magnus T. Bernhardsson, eds. London: I.B. Tauris & Co., 2002.

CHARISMATIC LEADERSHIP

Charismatic leaders are people who, by the use of emotional connection (charm, manipulation, etc.), communication style, or relational power are able to convince others to willingly follow them. Adherents typically perceive charismatic religious leaders to be uniquely imbued with divine power to lead others. Usually, these religious figures stand outside of conventional hierarchies and advocate for a radically different understanding of religion, often creating conflict with the religious establishment. While charismatic leadership can be a powerful and positive force for social change, it can also be manipulative, dangerous, and abusive.

Scholars have attempted to understand why charismatic leaders flourish and gain such loyal followers, in spite of the potential for manipulation and abuse. Sociologist Max Weber indicates that charismatic leadership depends on both the internal qualities of the leader ("gifts") as well as the acceptance of the group. When groups accept charismatic leaders, Weber contends, followers are willing to completely invest themselves in another person because of a deep need to overcome the constraints of their conventional world. Identification with someone who—through his or her gifts—seems able to transcend this world is a powerful motivator. Organizational psychologists who study contemporary business leaders note that loyalty often stems from the charismatic leader's unique ability to encourage high performance and group empowerment, which inspires further devotion and reverence in group members.

Unfortunately, the investment of followers in a charismatic leader can sometimes have disastrous or even deadly consequences. Hitler's rise to power following the detrimental effects of World War I on Germany is the most widely known example of a charismatic leader playing on the desire of the masses for radical change. The damage to Germany at that time, both architecturally (due to continuous bombing and artillery fire) and economically (due to reparations forced by the Treaty of Versailles), created a great sense of dissatisfaction and social unrest. In addition, the unstable socio-political climate meant that no solid government remained in power for longer than a few weeks at a time. This created an ideal setting for the takeover of a charismatic leader who promised great strength in recovery. The German population was so hungry for relief that Hitler's scapegoating of the Jews by arguing for their eradication seemed like a reasonable proposition, especially since the Jews had a long history of persecution. The offer of a solution to a seemingly impossible problem caused widespread support of Hitler and his agenda.

Another famous example of this dark side of charisma involves the Reverend Jim Jones and the mass suicide of People's Temple members at Jonestown. Jones inspired great loyalty in his followers based in part on his personal appeal and communication style, but also because of his ideologies, which promoted racial harmony and a coming age of reconciliation (see Maaga). However, Jones inspired such loyalty and was able to so heavily centralize his authority over group members that his followers lost any sense of self apart from the group and Jones himself. This was especially true once the group was isolated at the Jonestown, Guyana compound. When Jones claimed that the group was threatened, many members were willing to take their own lives at his behest rather than relinquish their investment in their leader.

However, all sides of charismatic leadership are not dark, nor is it only the domain of new religious movements. Traditional religions can also point to this influence, even at the time of their origins. In Judaism, the prophets of the Hebrew Bible were outside of the priestly class and depended instead on claims to direct divine guidance for their pronouncements (see Jeremiah 1:6–10 as an example). Similarly, in Christianity, the Apostle Paul asserted that his authority did not come from the disciples who had known the historical Jesus, but rather from a direct encounter with the risen Christ (Gal. 1:15–17). In Islam, the entire prophetic tradition is based on the belief that God gave direct revelation to humanity through a succession of prophets, ending with Muhammad, and then the continuing survival of Islam depended upon Muhammad's persuasive preaching and personality. More recently, Joseph Smith and his successor Brigham Young displayed charismatic leadership in the creation and establishment of Mormonism.

FOR FURTHER READING

Maaga, Mary McCormick. *Hearing the Voices of Jonestown*. Syracuse: Syracuse University Press, 1998.

Weber, Max. *On Charisma and Institution Building*. S.N. Eisenstadt, ed. Chicago: University of Chicago Press, 1968.

CONCLUSION

In spite of the audacity of our title, this is not everything you need to know about all religions, cults, or popular beliefs. First of all, everything you need to know would never fit in a book you would actually be able to lift off the shelf. More importantly, however, people change, and so do traditions. We have offered some (probably idealized) descriptions of belief systems, but the full range of meaning and practice for people in different periods and places can hardly be captured, here or elsewhere. For example, before the destruction of the second temple, Judaism may have been considered a religion that was connected solely to place, but the loss of the temple forced the religion to change. Beliefs constantly grow and change, so there is no way to include all elements of every religion in this book. Furthermore, there is no way to speak on behalf of over one billion Muslims or two billion Christians. Instead, we attempted to be as broad and encompassing as possible, and then to provide guidance on where to get more information if needed.

To that end, we hope you will utilize the "For Further Reading" section at the end of each article, which will offer additional books, popular websites, and news articles that further explain beliefs, events, and issues related to each religion or group. For any questions you might have that we do not address, talk about it. Ask people what they believe and how they understand the world. Ask pastors, priests, rabbis, congregation leaders, or teachers in your own community; these people and places can provide a wealth of information so that your interactions with people of different faiths will be more knowledgeable and respectful. You will come to have a stronger understanding of your own faith and be able to express yourself more clearly.

A final thought: in the introduction, we mentioned that we are both teachers, and that we have embarked on the adventure of writing this book to educate against ignorance and intolerance, and to spark understanding. For a teacher, there is no greater joy than seeing a student open her or his eyes to a bigger world and to bigger ideas. In sharing these religions, cults, and popular beliefs with you, we hope not only to inform you about names, dates, creeds, and texts. Instead, we want to be a part of that kind of eye-opening, mind-opening, respect-building enlightenment and understanding for all of you. It gives us hope.

CPSIA information can be obtained
at www.ICGtesting.com
Printed in the USA
LVHW091536171122
732977LV00006B/117